Pardoned or Paroled?

SANCTIFIED BY FAITH IN CHRIST

by Jefferis Kent Peterson

*"I am Jesus, whom you are persecuting. But rise and stand upon your feet; for I have appeared to you for this purpose, to appoint you to serve and bear witness to the things in which you have seen me and to those in which I will appear to you, delivering you from the people and from the Gentiles – to whom I send you to open their eyes, that they may turn from darkness to light and from the power of Satan to God, that they may receive forgiveness of sins and a place among those who are **sanctified by faith in me**." –Acts 26: 15-18*

Isaiah House Publishing
Erie, PA

© 1993 by Jefferis Kent Peterson &
© 2002 Jefferis Kent Peterson & Isaiah House Publishing, Erie, PA
All Rights Reserved
Printed in the United States of America

ISBN: 0-9718079-0-6
Isaiah House Publishing
PO Box 56
Erie, PA 16512-1152
USA

http://www.IS61.com
814-452-1152
ISPH@is61.com

No part of this book may be reproduced in any form without written permission of the publisher.
 The Bible text designated RSV is from The Holy Bible: Revised Standard Version. Copyright 1946, 1952, 1959, 1973 by the Division of Christian Education of the National Council of the Churches of Christ in the United States of America. All rights reserved. Used by permission.
 The Bible text designated NRSV is from The Holy Bible, New Revised Standard Version. Copyright 1989 by the Division of Christian Education of the National Council of the Churches of Christ in the United States of America. All rights reserved. Used by permission.
 The Bible text designated NASB is from The Holy Bible, NEW AMERICAN STANDARD BIBLE, (C) Copyright The Lockman Foundation 1960, 1962, 1963, 1968, 1971, 1972, 1973, 1975, 1977, 1995 Used by permission. All Rights Reserved - International Copyright Secured
 The Bible text designated NIV is from The Holy Bible, New International Version (R). Copyright (c) 1973, 1978, 1984 by International Bible Society. All rights reserved. Used by permission of Hodder Headline Plc.
 The Bible text designated KJV is from the the King James Version of the Bible.
 The Bible text designated NKJV is from The Holy Bible: New King James Version. Copyright (c) 1982 by Thomas Nelson, Inc. All rights reserved. Used by permission
 Undesignated Bible texts are the author's translation using The Greek New Testament, United Bible Society, Third Edition ©1975.

Cover art ©2002 by Peterson Design Studio (www.PetersonSales.net). Photo ©Hermera Technologies.

Dedication

This book is dedicated to the Lord Jesus Christ. May it bring You Glory, Lord, and bring healing to Your people!

Acknowledgements

I want to thank my wife, Leigh, for teaching me what to leave unsaid. Over the course of many years, you have helped me become a craftsman of the written word.

Many people read, advised, and encouraged me in the writing of this book. Among them are: Jim Kelly, who checked all my scripture references, Frank Parrish, Jim Baxter, Ed Bez, and John Weisman, who read it and gave me feedback. David Marin, who gave financial support and helped pay for my research! My Pastor, Jim Erb, who taught me about intimacy with God and who reminded me that in the Old Testament God is called, Yahweh M'Kadesh: God Who Sanctifies. Thank you all.

Mike and Kathy Bruno, thank you for your prayers.

Table of Contents

Introduction 1

Glossary 5

Chapter One: *Religious Witchcraft – The Trap of Legalism* 7

Chapter Two: *Sanctification – Christ's Completed Work In Us* 21

Chapter Three: *Sanctification and Righteous Conduct* 31

Chapter Four: *Sanctification – a Practical Application* 39

Chapter Five: *Laboring to Rest–Contrary Nature of Human Striving* 49

Chapter Six: *A Personal Testimony – The Spirit's Power* 71

Chapter Seven: *What is Faith?* 87

Chapter Eight: *What if I don't have enough faith?* 105

Chapter Nine: *Escaping the Trap of Lies* 113

Chapter Ten: *Faith Comes by Healing!* 119

Chapter Eleven: *The Goal of the Christian Life* 127

Chapter Twelve: *The Goal of Sanctification* 131

Chapter Thirteen: *God My Sanctifier* 135

Appendix: *A Summary Doctrine of Sanctification* 149

Academic Introduction

Read this section only if you are interested in current theological trends.

This book was written out of the struggle to find a relationship between the Protestant doctrine of "justification by faith" and sanctification, or right living, in Christ. It was a personal struggle because I wanted to know how to deal with the guilt of my continuing imperfection after coming to faith. I also wanted to learn to live a purified life, because I thought if I did, I would be able to do the works that Jesus did. I assumed that a life of miracles was a result of moral holiness. I read in the Scriptures that Jesus said, "He who believes in me will do the works that I do, and even greater works will he do ..." I was not performing miracles, and I wanted to do what I needed to make the promise of Scripture come to pass. So, I asked, "Now that I am saved by Christ's mercy, how good do I need to be, and how good can I be?"

Two current theological debates reflect the dynamics of my struggle and reveal that this issue is the same one which has troubled the Church for centuries. One debate is over the Reformation issue of "justification by faith," the other debate involves a doctrine called "Lordship Salvation." Recently, a dialog between Lutherans and Roman Catholics has asserted that much of the debate over the issue of justification by faith during the Reformation was due to a semantic misunderstanding. The Roman Catholic definition of justification is closer to the Protestant definition of sanctification – or righteous living after salvation. The fight was, in part, a result of confusion over the use of these two words. The two sides are said to agree that initial justification is indeed by grace through faith, and not by works. However, the Catholic view of sanctification, and its association with good works, seems to reignite the debate between faith and works in a new venue. This book deals with the subtle consequences of applying merit to one's performance of good deeds as well as to the confusion raised by the debate over "Lordship Salvation."

The debate in evangelical circles about the issue of "Lordship Salvation" has two basic positions. On one side, theologians like John MacArthur are rightly stating that unless our relationship to Christ produces some fruit of faith in our character and in our deeds, we have a reason to doubt whether we are really saved. To be "in Christ" is more than just believing that Jesus is the Son of God; it is allowing him to be "Lord" over our lives. Saving faith will be accompanied by a life of obedience, repentance, and submission. True, saving faith will have as its evidence the sanctification of our character. If these elements of transformation are lacking in us, it is possible that we do not have saving faith.[1]

On the other side of the debate, the traditional theologians of grace, like Charles Ryrie and Zane Hodges, are concerned about the effect the theology of Lordship Salvation will have on new Christians. Rather than causing us to trust Christ and his work, Lordship Theology will cause us to look to ourselves, and to our works and deeds, for some assurance of our salvation. Such a perspective is bound to make us miserable or extremely vain. Instead, these theologians present faith and salvation as God's free gift to us, regardless of how well we walk in paths of righteousness. Forgiveness covers our blunders, grace covers our weakness, and all the credit for our good deeds goes to God and God alone.

To explain the lack of evidence of salvation in some "believers," Ryrie and Hodges imply a two-tiered Christianity: while everyone who has faith in Jesus is God's child and is saved for eternity, not all of God's children are obedient. Just as is true in human families, in the family of God there are sons and daughters who listen to their Father's voice and obey, while some are still bent on following their selfish ways. Although still saved, these disobedient children are not growing towards maturity.[2]

Dr. Ryrie almost posits a dual class of kingdom citizenship. There are those who have received the free gift of salvation through faith in Christ by trusting in his mercy alone, and then there are

---

[1] *The Gospel According to Jesus*, by John F. MacArthur, © 1988 Academie Books, Grand Rapids, MI, pp. 32–33.

[2] *Absolutely Free*, by Zane Hodges, © 1989 by Rendencion Viva, Academie Books, Grand Rapids, MI, pp. 118, 132.

those who have gone beyond salvation and have accepted the call to be Christ's disciples. To be a disciple is to continually surrender more and more of one's own will, wants, and desires to Jesus as Lord and Master of life. This is the costly enterprise of discipleship. The prize is holiness, but not every Christian is willing to pay the price. Therein lies the difference between the first and second-class citizens, between the disciples and the mere believers.

Ryrie reassures us that even if we are of the second class of Christians – even though we are unwilling to render Jesus our obedience – if we have accepted Christ as savior, we have a place at the banquet table in the Kingdom of God. Salvation is indeed free; only discipleship is costly.[3]

While I value the contributions these brothers have made to the study of God's work in us, I believe they are confused about how sanctification actually works. By treating discipleship as a matter of our work instead of as a matter of faith, they make sanctification something to be achieved rather than something to be received! They miss the point that our sanctification is also by faith. It takes faith to walk in the perfection that God has purchased for us. *It is clear in the Scriptures that discipleship is not the means of our sanctification, but the fruit of it. We do not discipline ourselves and become holy enough to enter God's presence. We enter God's presence, become holy by fellowship with him, and so our flesh is disciplined!* The character of discipleship flows naturally out of a relationship with Jesus, but as soon as we look to our performance as a means to achieve our maturity, or as a means to measure our holiness, we take the focus off of what God has done for us in Jesus and put it on ourselves, our works, and our deeds. If we look to ourselves, there can never be faith!

Martin Luther struggled to know that he was truly saved in the face of his sinful nature. Even though he believed, he still sinned. In response to his quest for assurance, God gave Luther the revelation that he was saved by faith and faith alone. Upon that revelation, the whole Protestant world is founded. However, God, in His Word, said not only are we saved by faith; *we are sanctified by faith as*

---

[3] *So Great Salvation*, by Charles Ryrie, © 1989 SP Publications, Victor Books, Wheaton IL, pp. 74–76.

well! (Acts 26:18). We have to grasp this truth if we are to be set free from the nagging doubts and fears that attack us and cause us to question our salvation.

I would like to bring this debate out of the realm of the abstract down into a more personal discussion. It will be much less confusing and far more helpful. This whole issue has arisen because we have asked, "Although I believe in Jesus, my deeds are still evil. Am I doing enough to please God? Am I truly saved? If God has called me to be holy, why do I still live like this?" These questions are asked by those who want to know God better. They are questions of sanctification. "How can I be pure before God, have intimate fellowship with him, and walk before him unashamed?"

If you have ever asked yourself these questions, this book is for you. 🌿

GLOSSARY

Justification: see Righteousness

Holiness: see Sanctification

Righteousness (*dikaiosune*): in Greek the word means to stand up straight, to be upright, not crooked, or, by implication, to be in right standing with God. It implies that a person is completely conformed to the will of God in their life and that God is completely pleased because they have not sinned and do not sin. The word is also translated as *Justification,* which has a more judicial and legal sense, as in "declared not guilty" or "found innocent," by a court of law. But both *righteousness and justification* are translations of the same Greek word. Because we are not ever good enough to have earned such perfect standing with God, Paul says we have been given the "free gift of righteousness," (Romans 3:24, 5:17).

Sanctification (*hagiasmos*): in Greek the word means set apart for sacred use, the opposite of common, secular, and profane. The word is also translated as *Holiness.* The word *"saint"* also comes from the same word. Sanctification is often described as a purified character, which resembles the perfect character of God. It implies being holy and fit for God's use. Like righteousness, it means to be without spot or sin, but unlike righteousness, it is not just a judicial judgment of being declared innocent. Rather, it implies that a transformation of character has taken place so that a person is actually like Christ in personality, attitudes, and behavior. Often sanctification is described as a **process** whereby a person is becoming more and more like Jesus over time through repentance and yielding to the Holy Spirit. But the writers of the New Testament letters call even newborn babes in Christ *"saints"* – meaning the *"holy ones"* of God. Peter and Paul identify those who are in Christ as already possessing the character or virtue of holiness because of rebirth through the Holy Spirit.

Salvation (*soterion*): in Greek, and in the Hebrew, salvation means to save or deliver from enemies. It has a temporal meaning of saving from earthly circumstances like sickness, disease, stressful situations, poverty, and physical enemies. In fact, the word *"save"* (*sozo*) is actually translated "to heal" in many cases after Jesus heals the sick, as in "your faith has healed you (saved you)." The words are used interchangeably in Greek. *Salvation* also has an eternal implication as to a final deliverance from all the power of sin and death through spiritual rebirth now and finally in the resurrection:

"If you confess with your mouth, 'Jesus is Lord,' and believe in your heart that God raised him from the dead, you will be saved." —Romans 10:9, NIV

Chapter One

Religious Witchcraft – The Trap of Legalism

O foolish Galatians! Who has bewitched you, before whose eyes Jesus Christ was publicly portrayed as crucified? Let me ask you only this; did you receive the Spirit by works of the law, or by hearing with faith? Are you so foolish? Having begun with the Spirit, are you now ending with the flesh?
—Galatians 3: 1-3.

When a man is let out of prison on parole, he must be on his best behavior. He is assigned a parole officer. He must report to the officer on a regular basis. If he makes one mistake, he knows he can be thrown back into prison, so the parolee always lives with one eye over his shoulder, afraid that any misdeed or infraction of the rules might end his freedom. Sometimes, if he does not want to return to prison and has truly forsaken his life of crime, he will want to prove he has reformed by being on his best behavior, but he is still living in fear of making a mistake.

However, when a man is let out of prison on a pardon, no sword is hanging over his head. It is as if he had never committed any crime. He does not have to fear that a small mistake or slip up will return him to jail. He does not have to report to an officer and prove his goodness on a weekly basis. He can just go on about his life without ever looking back.

Christian guilt usually comes in two flavors. If you were raised in a strict, religious family, you may be walking around in a prison cell of fear – afraid of a thousand sins you might commit by sundown. You may be afraid of mortal sins, feeling guilty if you don't go to church every Sunday morning and Wednesday night. If you miss Bible study or Mass, you are sure you've committed another sin. No matter how good you try to be, your conscience is weighed down by a thousand transgressions. You live in fear of condemnation and in fear of God's constant displeasure.

Or if you are like me, you were not raised in church. You found a way to sin all on your own. The life you lived before you were in Christ makes you ashamed. There is nothing in my former life of which I am proud. In truth, upon coming to Christ, I was so ashamed of my pride and the way I lived, and so grateful for God's mercy, that I wanted to repay the Lord for his salvation. I wanted to be "super good." I wanted to do everything right and prove to the Lord that I wouldn't be bad anymore. I was like a man let out on parole. I really did not understand that my sins had been forgiven. I really did not understand what it meant to be pardoned.

I find a lot of Christians act like they are on parole. They walk on eggshells before God because they do not understand the forgiveness of God. They are always on their best behavior. There is a brittleness to their righteousness and a defensiveness to their faith. They are offended easily when someone does not receive their witness about Jesus. They feel compelled to "prove" Jesus is Lord and to "prove" their worthiness to God by "winning souls." Rather than resting in their confidence in God, they never seem to be able to relax. And they won't let you relax either. Have you ever met Christians who make you feel uneasy? I have. I was one of them. I was so self-righteous after I was saved that I was obnoxious. I was like the tattletale in school. I was full of zeal but lacking in grace. I was a parolee on his best behavior, but it wasn't the real me. I was driven by guilt and by fear of falling back into sin. I really didn't understand what it meant to be set free from sin's reminder. I was trying to pay back my Savior for my former ignorance. What an impossible load! Well, after a couple of months of that foolishness, I gave up on trying to perfect myself. It wasn't working anyway. I was only becoming miserably aware of my shortcomings. At that point, I began my long quest to find a more secure foundation for my acceptance in Christ than the foundation built on my own "good" behavior.

When I was first saved, I had a lot of help in being "religiously weird." I received a lot of advice from other Christians. I should say, it was not when I was *first* saved that I became unbearable, because when I was first saved, for the first few months of my sophomore year of college, all I did was skip class, read the Bible, pray, give thanks to God, and enjoy the love and presence of Jesus. I was having fun before the Lord and enjoying him. But shortly after that honeymoon of friendship with Jesus, I was told that in order to be a "good" Christian I needed to have a "quiet time" every day of at least an hour, and I "needed" to read my bible everyday. And if I really wanted to be pleasing to God, I needed to lead someone else to the Lord once a week.

Do you know what happened when all this legalistic advice came forth? It crushed my joy! It made a burden of what had been a pleasure. It made a duty and a chore of what before had been pure joy! Now, under the threat of punishment, failure, and the Father's displeasure, I had better have that quiet time or else ...or else, God wouldn't love me as much ...at least that was the implication. And suddenly, I found myself on the treadmill of proving that I was indeed a new person and an obedient child of God. I had been ...let out on parole ...

Now, mind you, it wasn't just young brothers and sisters in the Lord who were misleading me with good intentions. I was receiving this message from people who should have known better ...from adult leaders of our college campus youth ministry. But the result of all their "advice" was that now I hated to read my bible; it was such a burden. I felt rejected by God every time I tried to enter his presence in the "quiet place," because no matter how much time I read the Word or spent with him, I always felt it wasn't enough. I should do more. "How much is enough to be pleasing to God?" That was the question which caused my inner struggles. The easy relationship I had with my Lord was cut off. A painful chasm had developed in our friendship, and I was to blame – or so my mind said.

Generations of Christians have been plagued by this feeling of separation between themselves and the Lord. This struggle to become a "good" person and to be more like Christ has been an issue for the Church for thousands of years. Very few people are able simply to enjoy God's presence without being bothered by guilt and a sense of failure. We all see the image of the perfect love of God in Jesus, and we are all aware of how we fail to live like Jesus. We see what we are and we also see what we should be, and it bothers our conscience. The Bible gives us instructions on how to live a godly and holy life, but our ability to follow the pattern set out for us is weak. We often fail to carry out the simplest commands of Jesus. We may pray, for example, but we still become so easily annoyed with others that our anger and irritation reveal how far we are from the Lord.

It is this awareness of our failings that has caused this struggle of conscience for believers throughout the ages. We all want to know how to become more like Jesus. The Western Church calls this process of growth into the likeness of Jesus "sanctification." We seem to have a vision of the goal, but most us fail in our attempts to be like Him. Some people have separated themselves from the world out of a desire to be like Christ. Some have become ascetic hermits, seeking holiness in a life of poverty and isolation. Others have entered monasteries, seeking to become like Christ through a life of simplicity, contemplation, and prayer. Some have the misconception that you could be holy only if you denied yourself marriage and worldly goods, and so they retreated from the world out of a fear of being tainted by it.

It was out of this fear that Martin Luther entered a monastery and began to study the Scriptures in the early 1500's, but Martin Luther found that his desire for assurance before God was not satisfied. No matter how many times he prayed or repented, his fear remained. It was this fear of God and his struggle to know that he was doing enough to please God that finally caused Luther to abandon any attempts to find security in his good works or in his piety. Luther saw how pitiful his religious behavior was, and he cried out to God for some other assurance of God's love and favor. In response, God gave Martin Luther an understanding that a man was justified by "faith alone,"[4] and not by works. This revelation of truth spawned the whole Protestant Reformation. People began to realize that God did not condemn them: they were free from the debt of sin through their faith in Jesus Christ. They did not have to say endless prayers of confession or do penance to escape hell because Jesus had already paid the price for their sins. They were saved by Christ's work, not by their own. Christ's work on the cross was enough.

After Martin Luther, people began to ask other questions, "Now that I am saved, what next? Do I just continue to sin, or does God expect me to become sinless like Jesus? " John Calvin, a French Protestant who helped start the Presbyterian and Reformed Churches, believed that the Law of God revealed in the Scriptures was to be a guide to Christian behavior after salvation. He agreed with Luther that the Law revealed our sinful state and our need for God's mercy, but he added, that once the Holy Spirit has been given to a new Christian, the Law should teach you how to live. Calvin defined sanctification as the gradual growth of our character and our behavior into godliness. The Law existed to direct us in that growth. Neither Calvin nor Luther could tell us exactly how we would become more like Christ, but both agreed that should be our goal. Neither believed we would be perfect until Christ returned to the earth. Both Calvin and Luther believed that we would continue to sin and always need forgiveness, but Calvin had more hope in the potential reform of human nature than did Luther. Calvin believed that we would become more like Jesus the longer we lived and followed him.

Calvin's hope for our sanctification led to another set of questions: "How holy does God expect us to become? And what happens if I fail to live up to this expectation? Will I lose my salvation?" John Wesley, who lived 200 years after Luther and Calvin, was not content with the seeming contradiction created by them. He wondered, "How can we hope for sanctification if we will always continue to sin and be sinful?" He saw that the Bible held out hope for an ever-increasing righteousness in us with the

---

[4] Romans 1: 16– 17; 3: 21– 30

possibility of freedom from all sin. He noted that the First Letter of John talks about mature believers who are "made perfect in love" and who "do not sin."[5] Wesley reasoned that there must be more to believing than simply asking for forgiveness; "Entire Sanctification" from all sin must be possible even now in this life. John Wesley taught this sanctifying work of the Holy Spirit as a "second work of Grace." While he never claimed to have achieved sinless perfection, he did experience the power and personal presence of God in a new way. That experience is often called being "baptized with the Holy Spirit" in Pentecostal and Charismatic circles today and is a common experience throughout the Church among members of every denomination. It has not, however, produced a sinless state of perfection for believers.

Joy in Holiness or Laboring in the Flesh

So still today, the questions raised by Luther, Calvin, and Wesley continue to cause a struggle in the heart of almost every Christian. We want to know if we are living up to what God expects of us, but we do not know how do it. *The proper answer to this question of our sanctification is the key to Christian liberty. The wrong answer brings religious bondage.* If we fail to understand how sanctification actually takes place in us, we will be strongly tempted to turn away from Christ and fall back into a pattern of performance, trying to achieve holiness through our good deeds. Such self-made holiness is absolutely contrary to God's methods. In fact, Paul calls this attempt at self-perfection a counterfeit of God's true holiness and a form of spiritual witchcraft.[6] It is a deception. He says if we are deceived by it and turn away from our faith in Christ to works of human effort, we will be cut off from grace!

> *For all who rely on the works of the law are under a curse; for it is written, "Cursed is everyone who does not observe and obey all the things written in the book of the law." Now it is evident that no one is justified before God by the law; for*

---

[5] 1 John 3:4–6 ; 4:18
[6] Galatians 3: 1–3

"The one who is righteous will live by faith."
–Galatians 3:10-11, NRSV

You who want to be justified by the law have cut yourselves off from Christ; you have fallen away from grace.
–Galatians 5:4, NRSV

Paul also says that when we turn from God's grace to the Law, it will kill our joy! (Cf. Gal 4:15) That surely explains why I lost my joy as a young believer. Somewhere, somehow I turned from a simple trust in Jesus to a false trust in my own efforts to be good.

There is indeed a right and wrong way to seek holiness. Luther was right: we are saved by faith and not by works. Calvin was right: the Law exists to reveal our sin and the goal of sanctification. Wesley was also right: complete sanctification and perfection in love are possible in this life, but not through our strength and moral character. Our sanctification is possible because Jesus Christ, our Sanctifier, lives in us! We are not holy, but Christ, who lives in us is! *The danger is that instead of trusting Christ to sanctify us, we will seek to sanctify ourselves through good behavior and so fall prey to the deceptions of spiritual witchcraft.* One of the ways we fall prey to deception is that we seek to sanctify ourselves through the religious lure of *false piety*.

I have come to hate false piety, not because spending time with the Lord in prayer and worship is a bad thing to do, but because the motive is what really matters. If you are having a quiet time or going to church to be a "good" Christian, then you are deceived. If you spend hours in prayer trying to be pleasing to God, then you are on the wrong track. It is not the hours you spend in prayer that matter but the faith with which you pray! A short prayer, full of faith, is better than long hours of unbelieving petition and intercession. Jesus said that the Gentiles think they are heard for their long-winded prayers, but then he said, we are not to pray like them. He also criticized the hypocrites, who prayed three times a day out on the street corner to show how holy they were to other men. He said, they already have their reward.[7] Do you know how to tell if you believe God when you pray? You'll know you have faith

---

[7] Matthew. 6:5–8

if you have confidence that the Father hears your prayers.[8]

Being Religious or Trusting God

It has been a hard struggle for me to escape the snare of religious behavior. It has taken years to get back to the simplicity of my first love. I tell you, I did not return to the simple joy of resting in the presence of Jesus and of reading his Word by any religious discipline! On the contrary, only by rejecting that religious mentality have I been able to return to the simple joy that faith produces. It is this ongoing battle with conventional wisdom which motivated me to write this book. I would like to spare you the troubles I have experienced, if at all possible. For this reason, I am attacking a false understanding of sanctification.

My beloved wife, who put up with me through all my struggles to return to the simple faith of a newborn Christian, reminded me of all the contortions I have gone through on my "religious" quest to know Jesus better. Although I understood the principle of grace with my mind, I could not shake the nagging feeling that I was not "doing" enough to please God. Guilt and fear of failure grasped my soul like a millstone, dragging me down. Although I despaired of pleasing Christ because I could see my sinful attitudes, thoughts, and desires, I would continually venture out on some new course of obedience:

After listening to a teaching on prayer, for example, I began to pray the Lord's Prayer. My prayer life expanded dramatically. I became much more balanced in my prayers, not centering on my needs but on Christ's will. I would arise at 4 a.m. and pray until 8:00 a.m., praying for all the needs of the earth. For a season, I really was strengthened in my relationship to God. But soon what was a teaching became a rote pattern of behavior, devoid of faith. Now I *had* to pray every day. I was no longer approaching God in faith, but I felt as if I had found "my calling" and suddenly, it became a duty. There was no longer any faith involved in my actions. It degenerated into a religious obligation, and when I did not pray every day, I felt guilty.

---
[8] 1 John 5:14

While this life of prayer went on for months, it became arid and empty. Finally, after crying out to God, "Why isn't this working like it used to?" I sensed God saying to me, "Cease striving and know that I am God," (Psalm 46: 10, ASV). God was not calling me to rote, religious behavior, but to rest in his presence. For a season, I did rest, but I couldn't really believe that was all God wanted me to do. I felt I should be doing something more, and guilt crept back in. So soon, I was off on another religious quest...

The next endeavor was praise and worship. I would sing songs of praise and worship to God for about four hours each day, and indeed, I would bask in his presence and enjoy God. But after several months, that too became something I felt "I needed to do" to be pleasing to God. What was joy soon became religion. The life went out of it. Again, the guilt returned. Again, I cried out, "Why isn't this working?" And again, God spoke in my heart, "Jeff, you are trying to perform for me, but I have called you to rest in me."

This pattern repeated itself over and over again through the years, and each time God would conclude my efforts with the call to trust in him, *but I couldn't believe it!* I couldn't believe his requirements for obedience were that simple! So, after a few weeks of rest, I would stray back into some effort to fulfill God's plan for my life.

The hardest of all callings is to trust God so much that rather than do anything to earn his favor you simply rest in his love. Yet that is the message of faith: Jesus has paid the price for our sanctification. Our highest calling is to trust the Father like Jesus does. While he was on the earth, Jesus did not strive in his relationship with the Father. He did not fear that the Father would condemn him, but he continually trusted the Father. Out of his "rest" in the Father, great power was released! So may it be for us as well, that as we rest in him, we may do the works that he did.

Normally, I am not willing to argue with other Christians over doctrines because they are usually fights over minor matters that are not essential to our salvation in Christ. Besides, you can have all the right doctrines and still be wrong in your attitude toward your brother. The Pharisees were right in their doctrines about the resurrection, but they hated Jesus! And we are not saved by our intellectual knowledge of doctrine but by our trust in Jesus and in his sacrifice for us on the cross! Even if we are wrong in some of our doctrines, if we believe that Christ died and was raised for us, then the Lord's love will cover a multitude of our sins and make up for many of our errors in thinking. Although I won't usually fight over doctrines, this is one case where I feel compelled to take a stand and risk making enemies. For what you hold about the doctrine of sanctification makes all the difference in the world. It is the difference between a joy-filled, thankful life of faith and a life of bitterness driven by feelings of failure. For that reason, I hope to prescribe some sound doctrine as a medicine for your soul.

Witchcraft or Holiness

A false understanding of sanctification leads to all manner of sinful deeds and deceptions. One of the greatest crimes that can be committed against our faith is the attempt to find some form of righteousness within ourselves. It is this spirit of legalism, arising from a misunderstanding of holiness, which robbed me of my joy in the Lord. This legalism is the very same spirit Paul was constantly fighting in his churches. Paul called those who attacked his Gospel of righteousness by faith "workers of iniquity, false apostles, and Satan's servants who pretend to be holy and righteous."[9] These people introduced many outward forms of religious exercise, and they called the people to a more rigorous devotion to right living in order to "prove" their salvation. Paul called their effort to "sanctify" themselves after salvation through good works a form of witchcraft!

"Who has bewitched you?" he says. *"What righteousness did you have that got you saved? You didn't have any! So, what got you saved? Some good deed on your part? No! You were saved because you believed the message you heard about Jesus!"*[10] *"Now,"* says Paul,

---
[9] 2 Corinthians 11: 12–15

"having begun in the Spirit with faith, are you trying to perfect yourself through another means; the strength of your flesh?" In other words, are you trying to sanctify yourself by being a "good" Christian? Aaaagh! It won't work! If you want to be sanctified, if you want to complete the work of the Spirit in you, then you will have to finish the race the same way you started! By faith! It is faith that got you saved, and it is faith that will bring you sanctification as well. Faith will complete the work of God in you: nothing more and nothing less! No good deeds, no pious behavior, no amount of reading the bible or hours of prayer will fill the gap in your personality or end the deficit of your character.

But "Faith in what?" you might ask. Faith in Jesus: faith in his finished work on the cross! Faith that what Jesus did to save you is sufficient to sanctify you as well. You see, we are not sanctified by our good deeds, but by Christ's act of obedience, and as we trust in Jesus' sacrifice, the Holiness of God is revealed in us. We are sanctified by Jesus, and a mature faith will allow us to rest fully in Christ's finished work. I will speak more about this later, but for now, let me give you a foretaste: if we try to add anything to the cross, like some good deed or effort on our part, we are saying, in effect, "The sacrifice of Jesus was not enough for me. What he did on the cross was not good enough to save me or to satisfy God. I have to do this work in order to be saved and sanctified. My salvation does not depend upon Christ, but upon how good I can be." That line of thought is deception, for then our trust rests not in Christ but in ourselves and in our efforts. We become the focus for our salvation and Jesus becomes peripheral to us. Our sanctification depends upon how good we can be and not upon Jesus. *How perverse can we be to think that there would ever be found any goodness in us worthy of fellowship with God!*

Look, my friends, the truth is that we have no righteousness within us and we never will. It is a mistake to look for some kind of righteousness in our personality or character. It is the height of pride to think that some pious behavior or good deed on our part would make us worthy to approach the Almighty God. The Lord said

---

[10] Galatians 3: 1–3

in Isaiah, *"Only in the Lord, it shall be said of me, are righteousness and strength,"* (Isaiah 45:24, RSV). Only God is righteous! Only God is good! So, it is crazy for us to seek our sanctification in some outward act or good deed. Our sanctification, like our righteousness, is in the Lord. Our sanctification and our righteousness is the Holy Spirit dwelling in us. It is the presence of God in us, and we receive our righteousness as a gift[11] from God, because God himself is the gift. In fact, we first receive his righteous presence within us when we are willing to acknowledge our need for a Savior, for we only begin to rely upon God's righteousness when we realize we cannot save ourselves. When we acknowledge that we are not righteous, but that Jesus Christ is, we are finally starting to see ourselves in a clear light. We finally start to trust God's righteousness because we see we cannot trust our own.

From Faith to Sinlessness

Let me tell you about a mystery of God's goodness towards us. In Romans, Paul says that our faith is "counted as righteousness," and that God does not count the sin of the one who believes in Jesus Christ (Romans 4: 5-7). In other words, when you believe in Jesus, in God's eyes *it is as if you have never sinned!* When we admit that we are not good, but confess that Jesus Christ is good, God looks upon us as if we too had perfectly obeyed him and gone to the cross without sin![12] Jesus' obedience becomes a substitute for ours, and God the Father looks upon us as if we had perfectly obeyed him. *What else can we do then to gain God's favor if already we are without sin in his sight? What sacrifice can we add?*

Now not only have we received God's righteousness through our trust in Christ, Jesus said that we receive our sanctification the same way: by faith in him![13] Actually, if we grasp the simple truth that Jesus is our righteousness, and we do not have to earn righteousness, we are set free! A great weight is lifted off our shoulders. We do not have to perform for God. We are not out on parole, but truly pardoned. If we grasp this truth, gratitude will replace fear; thanksgiving will replace worry; and the joy of the

---

[11] Romans 5:17

[12] Romans 4; especially "For what saith the Scripture? Abraham believed God, and it was counted unto him for righteousness." (Romans 4:3, KJV)

[13] Acts 26:18

Lord will make the character of Christ shine out from our hearts. All we do is believe that **he** is righteous and trust him to make us like himself, and this faith will produce the character of Christ in us – which is in our sanctification! *So, my friends, it is faith from beginning to end! Faith for salvation, faith for righteousness, and faith for sanctification.*

I know that if my experience has struck a chord in your heart, you have felt the pain of feeling distant from God at times as well. You have been aware of an awful sense of unworthiness before the throne of God's majesty. You have felt anxiety. You wonder how to overcome the guilt and enter in to intimacy with God. Trusting Christ for your sanctification, I guarantee you, is the bridge over the troubled waters of your heart to the "Rest" of the promised land of God's presence ... ❦

CHAPTER TWO

SANCTIFICATION: CHRIST'S COMPLETED WORK IN US

*Consequently, when Christ came into the world, he said, "Sacrifices and offerings thou hast not desired, but a body hast thou prepared for me; in burnt offerings and sin offerings thou hast taken no pleasure. Then I said, 'Lo, I have come to do thy will, O God,' as is written of me in the roll of the book." When he said above, "Thou hast neither desired nor taken pleasure in sacrifices and offerings ..." then he added, "Lo, I have come to do thy will." He abolishes the first (covenant) in order to establish the second. And by that will **we have been sanctified** through the offering of the body of Jesus Christ, once for all ... For by a single offering he has perfected for all time those who are sanctified.*
–Hebrews 10: 5-10,14, RSV

It may be hard for you to believe that your sanctification is already complete in Christ, so I want to show you the truth from the Word of God. As it says in Hebrews, we have been sanctified and perfected for all time through the obedient sacrifice of Jesus. The *New International Version* does not translate these verses correctly. The tense of the Greek verbs in this text is the "aorist" tense, which describes a completed action, not an ongoing action. It is correctly translated by the *Revised Standard Version* as something that happened in the past: "we have been sanctified."

The Word of God is saying that by offering his body on the cross, Jesus not only paid for our sins but sanctified us as well! *He made us perfect and holy in the eyes of God.* He completed our sanctification in holiness forever through that sacrifice, and there is not one thing we can add to his sacrifice to increase our level of holiness or sanctification. It is finished! Whenever we try to become sanctified by any other means, we enter into deception, because we try to gain through our labors what has already been freely given us in Christ. Rather than turn to Christ to receive of him, we turn to ourselves to work our way into his holy presence.

Satan's chief deception is to make us forget the benefits of Christ so that we will try to add to the cross some work of our own. We suppose we can make up for what Christ has failed to do for us. Do you see what is at stake here? If we do not accept Jesus' sacrifice as sufficient to purchase our salvation *and* our sanctification, we fall back under the spell of bewitchment. Instead of trusting Jesus and the Holy Spirit to finish the work in us, we turn to something we might do as humans to attain holiness, not realizing Jesus is our answer!

The "Work" of Sanctification is Believing

If there is any work of sanctification on our part, it is merely this: that we learn to discern between the devil's lies and the truth of Christ. The devil wishes to divide us from our trust in Christ and make us believe that we are lacking something. He wants us to believe that Christ's work on the cross was not enough, so that we will turn again to the dead works of human nature. The "process" of sanctification, then, is simply to put to death this deception of the devil, which robs us of our peace with God.

Do you not think it strange, that when you strive to be a "good" Christian, rather than finding peace, you find instead that all kinds of fear, anxiety, irritation, and stress in your life? Why does that happen? It happens because we know in our hearts we are sinful and unworthy of God. When we compare our acts and deeds and the thoughts of our hearts to God's perfect, holy, and righteous standard, we always fall short. So, if we measure our holiness by our performance, we will always have a reason to be depressed! "No one is righteous, no not one!" says the Word, and that is true. There is nothing in us that could hope to give us confidence before God that we are living right. So, sanctification cannot possibly be something we achieve through our efforts. We cannot complete the work of faith through the strength of our flesh or the power of our human nature, as Paul pointed out. So, how then can we be obedient? How can we be pleasing to God?

I am going to make an astounding statement here. If we wish to be obedient to Christ, there is only one thing that God requires of us: *believe in Jesus' sufficiency to save us, cleanse us, purify us, and make us whole.* It is our faith in him which pleases God. To add any other work to this work of faith is to deny the sufficiency of the cross. It is saying to God "Jesus isn't enough."

If we trust Christ's work on the cross and stop trying to make ourselves righteous, holy, and acceptable to God – *we then begin to walk in true faith.* It is through our trust in Jesus that we receive God's gift of holiness. If we abide and dwell in his presence, his nature begins to shine through us, not through some effort on our part, but because God is with us. We cease striving and rest in him, and the grace of his character is allowed to mold and conform our image to his. Therefore, our sole work is to believe what Jesus has done for us and to cease from our labors, so that we might partake of the benefits of his sacrifice and become like him.[14]

Sanctification is a Matter of the Heart

The major stumbling block most of us have to sanctification is that we try to attain holiness through some work of our own. However, an outward act of "righteousness," like tithing or time spent in prayer, will not bring sanctification to us. Yes, there is a "process" whereby we absorb God's sanctification of our character. Yes, a sanctified character will produce evidence of Christ's likeness in specific acts and deeds; but these aspects of attitude and action will only reveal what has already taken place in us through our relationship with Jesus. *They are not the means to gain that relationship of intimacy. They are the evidence that this relationship, built on trust, already exists!*

And what does it mean to be like Christ? Does it mean that we

---

[14] Then said they unto him, What shall we do, that we might work the works of God? Jesus answered and said unto them, This is the work of God, that ye believe on him whom he hath sent. (John 6:28– 29, KJV) There remaineth therefore a rest to the people of God. For he that is entered into his rest, he also hath ceased from his own works, as God did from his. (Hebrews 4:9 – 10, KJV)

never fail or sin? Does it mean that we follow the law perfectly? I wish that were true! Being holy is more than simply not making mistakes. It is more than outward actions; it is an inner attitude of the heart. Most people view holiness as some outward sign of behavior like not swearing, not drinking, not smoking, not going to movies, not wearing makeup, and women not wearing pants! The Pharisees were very good at showing an external form of righteousness, but Jesus called them "whitewashed tombs," because, while in outward appearance they were very righteous, inside they were full of envy, jealousy, bitterness, judgment, and hatred. They were evil in heart. They were not moved by love and compassion but by a critical spirit. How many "good" Christians do you know who appear to live good lives, but who are full of anger towards the world and sinners? I've had a tendency at times to be more angry about sin than joyous in the Lord. Then I have to ask myself, "Why don't I love the sinner, like Jesus does?"

Jesus was different. He was grieved by sin, but he loved the sinner. Jesus loved the poor, the lame, the sick, the downcast, and the outcast. He had mercy upon the prostitute and the criminal. He did not judge them but forgave them. Our righteousness, our sanctification, is indeed to be like Christ, but rather than some outward form of religion, our hearts are to be conformed to his. Our character will resemble his as we live out our sanctification. When we realize that we have no excuse, but have sinned and been saved by the grace of God; then we will show mercy and kindness to others. We will be forgiving of the sins and failings of others. Don't you see? *That* is how the sanctification of our character is revealed: through our mercy, our love, our compassion; and not through some rigid outward obedience to a law. As we become more loving and merciful towards others, we become more like God.

A Code of Conduct or an Expression of Identity?

When I first received Jesus as my Lord and Savior, I used to read Galatians 5: 16-26 as a laundry list of *do's and don'ts*. If you want to be a good Christian, then you will do this and this and this, but if you are a bad Christian then you won't:

> *So I say to you, "Walk in the Spirit, and you will not fulfill the desires of the flesh." For the flesh desires what is contrary to the Spirit, and the Spirit what is contrary to the flesh: and these are in conflict with each other so that you will not do what you want. But if you are led by the Spirit, you are not under the law. Now the works the flesh produce are clear, like adultery, fornication, sexual impurity and debauchery; idolatry, witchcraft, hatred, discord, jealousy, fits of anger and rage, selfishness, factions, party spirit; envy, murder, drunkenness, carousing, and the like. Like I told you before, as I tell you now, those who continue in such things will not inherit the kingdom of God. But the fruit of the Spirit is love, joy, peace, endurance, gentleness, goodness, humility, faith, and self-control: against such things there is no law. And everyone who belongs to Christ has crucified the flesh with its impulsive passions and compulsive desires. If we live in the Spirit, let us also walk in the Spirit. Let us not seek our own glory, provoking each other, or yield to a competitive spirit. –Galatians 5:16-26*

I was mistaken about the meaning of this passage. It is not a code of conduct which must be followed in order to be a good Christian – like some New Testament Law – this scripture is more like a signpost revealing where you are in your walk of faith. If you are in faith and in the Spirit, *then* these works will be evident in your character: love, kindness, gentleness, etc. But if you are not in faith, if you are out of the Spirit, *then* these acts and attitudes will be evident: hatred, anger, jealousy, drunkenness, etc. You may be giving your tithe. You may be praying three times a day. You may go to church religiously and never miss a Sunday; but if you are jealous or angry with someone in your heart, then that signpost reveals you are out of the Spirit: you are not walking by faith; you have slipped back into works and self-trust! As soon as you fall from faith, those judgmental attitudes will creep back into your character. Those attitudes are signposts.

Conversely, if we are resting in grace and trusting Jesus for our righteousness and sanctification, then we will have peace before God. When we contemplate the gap between *who we are and who we ought to be,* we will no longer be agitated and afraid. Instead, we will cling more dearly to Jesus with gratitude because we know how much we have been forgiven. As we rest in his mercy towards us, his love will wash away the unclean attitudes and fears in our hearts. Instead of striving to be perfect, we will be thankful to God. Instead of being angry and hostile towards others when they fail, we will extend to them that same mercy we have received. *The fruit of the Spirit will be revealed in us, not because we are living right, but because we have abandoned our attempts to be right! We have let Christ be right for us!* The character of Jesus will be revealed in us because we are walking the walk of faith in him instead of walking in our "good" works. We will be trusting Jesus and not ourselves.

The Object of Our Attention

We all want to manifest the character of Christ. We all want to be more like him, but how does that happen? How does the maturity of the Holy Spirit manifest the fruit of his nature in us and through us? It says in the Scriptures that we come to resemble what occupies our attention . If we look to ourselves, with our weakness, frailty, failure, and sin, then we will be conformed to the image of our failure. If we spend all day in front of the television set watching problems, both real and imagined, the bad "news" of the day, the pornography and infidelity of the shows of titillation, then we will be conformed to those images. Whatever affixes our gaze will lay hold of our personality, and through endless contemplation on those things, we will reflect their character, whether good or evil. But Paul says, "Whatever is good and holy, think on these things," (Philippians 4:8). Why? Because our mind, our personality, our soul is renewed through a daily application of the truth of God: "And do not be conformed to this world: but be transformed by the renewal of your mind, that you may prove what is the will of God," (Romans 12:2, RSV).

We are transformed, Paul says, not by endless attempts to perfect ourselves, but by forgetting about ourselves and fixing our attention upon Jesus:

> *And we all, with unveiled face, beholding the glory of the Lord, are being changed into his likeness from one degree of glory to another; for this comes by the Lord who is the Spirit.*
> *–2 Corinthians 3:18, RSV.*

By fixing our attention upon Jesus, we become like him and sin loses its hold upon us. When Moses gazed upon God on Mount Sinai and spent time in God's presence, Moses came down from the mountain with his own face shining white as he reflected the glory of God. Paul says the same thing will happen to us as we gaze at Jesus. Just as Jesus was transfigured on the mountain as he had fellowship with the Father, so also our faces will reflect that same glory as we are engaged in his presence.[15] Our image is conformed to the object of our rapt attention.

What foolishness it is then to think that we could clean ourselves up enough to enter the presence of God! *We don't sanctify ourselves and enter his presence; we enter his presence and his presence sanctifies us!* We don't sanctify ourselves enough to become worthy to enter through the veil into the Holy of Holies. That will never happen! The blood of Jesus washes us, and we enter the Holy of Holies because he has cleansed us. Then this intimate fellowship with God in the Holy of Holies produces a sanctified character in us. We resemble Jesus not because of our labors but because of our fellowship with him. Our character is transformed to be like his through the love we receive from him. We become partakers of his glory, and his glory works its effects in our lives.

Our Perfection is Love, not Labor

How different is God's way from our natural inclination to perform some work of self-perfection! Faith that produces change

---

[15] Matthew 17:2; Exodus 34:29

in us and sanctifies us is not some abstract theological concept. The faith that makes us whole is a relationship! That is why the promotion of "quiet times," bible study, and church attendance is such a weak counterfeit to true righteousness. A simple list of *do's and don'ts* will not substitute for what God is really trying to do in us. God wants to conform us to the image of his dear Son, not produce a bunch of little religious robots! We are talking here about the difference between religious legalism and *faith*, which pleases God. The great gift of God's righteousness cannot be reduced to a set of rules because his righteousness is expressed to us through and by Love. *His Righteousness is Love.* His righteousness is expressed through us as we walk with him. Our righteousness is a reflection of a living, breathing relationship of love with God. It is God in our midst who brings his righteousness to us and through us. Since love is a relationship between us, it cannot be reduced to a list of rules and regulations.

Jesus said that we are made perfect by loving our enemies,[16] and that loving God and loving our neighbors are the greatest commandments of the law.[17] For this reason, Paul says, love is the fulfillment of the law.[18] The only New Testament commandment that Jesus gives is that we "love one another," as he loves us, (John 13:34). If we are going to be sanctified, it is not by religious duty, but by love. Loving others will be the sign of our perfection and sanctification in God.[19] What religious duty can you perform that will make you love your enemies?

You cannot regulate love. You cannot force love to happen. Love, by its very nature, is an act of a free will. It can be a response, but it can never be forced. It can only be given freely. Certain things may reveal whether or not you are in love, but no set of rules will produce love in you. For example, if you love your spouse, you may bring her roses just because you love her, but you could bring her roses every day for a month trying to make yourself love her, and it would not change your heart! In fact, you would probably

---

[16] Matthew 5:43-48

[17] Matthew 22:36-40

[18] Romans 13:8-10

[19] There is no fear in love, but perfect love casts out fear. For fear has to do with punishment, and he who fears is not perfected in love. (1John 4:18)

grow resentful if you had to continually bring her flowers. The duty would not make you love but would make you angry.

Love, like righteousness, comes from the heart, not from some external act. A man may not commit adultery, a man may be faithful according to the external requirements of God's law, but no law can cause a man to love his wife from his heart. Only something that is inexplicable and free produces love. Only something that comes from within, un-coerced, can fulfill the spirit of the law. In the same way, our sanctification comes out of relationship. It is akin to love, and love enables it to become a reality in our lives. It cannot be forced upon us, and no letter of the law will produce it. No set of standards or code of behavior will bring it to pass. Paul rightly said, "The Spirit gives life, but the letter kills." So, to reduce the work of God in our lives to a quiet time or long hours of prayer is to make a mockery of the Spirit of God. It is like putting our relationship to God on some kind of checklist of daily chores. It cannot happen!

The effect of sanctification on our character is the image of Christ being reflected in us and through us. This sanctification, purchased for us by Jesus on the cross, is revealed in us as we grow close to him. Our gazing upon him and forgetting ourselves, and our intimacy with him through faith, all work to produce the likeness of Christ in us. As it says, "He is the source of your life in Christ Jesus, whom God made our wisdom, *our righteousness and sanctification* and redemption." [20] As we cling to him in love, his righteous nature flows out of us as naturally as water flows downstream. Our deeds will begin to reflect God's goodness. It is the embrace of Christ's love that causes us to be conformed to his image. When that easy embrace happens, our faith is firmly fixed on Jesus and we are freed from self-concern. When that happens, we have escaped the spell of witchcraft and are set free to walk in the Spirit by his grace.

---

[20] 1 Cor. 1:30, (RSV)

Chapter Three

Sanctification and Righteous Conduct

And to whom did he swear that they should never enter his rest, but to those who were disobedient? So we see that they were unable to enter because of unbelief ...So then, there remains a Sabbath rest for the people of God; for whoever enters God's rest also ceases from his labors as God did from his. Let us labor to enter that rest, so that no one fall by the same sort of disobedience. –Hebrews 3:18-19; 4:9-11, RSV

I suppose it might seem glib of me to suggest that sanctification, like salvation, is by faith. I can just hear your questions: "What about gross sins like adultery and fornication and homosexuality? Doesn't sanctification include quitting those things? How can you say 'faith is obedience,' if someone believes in Jesus, but is still stealing or using drugs? Are they sanctified? Is 'faith' a substitute for right living?"

How did Paul address the Corinthians – that group of backbiting, schismatic, proud and boastful people who were so tolerant of sexual immorality in their midst? He said, "To the church of God which is at Corinth, to those *sanctified* in Christ Jesus, called to be saints together with all those who in every place call on the name of our Lord Jesus Christ, both their Lord and ours," (1 Corinthians 1:2, RSV). Paul was speaking to the Corinthians as new creatures in Christ Jesus, not according to their behavior in the flesh. In other letters, he calls the Christians "saints," even though they still have many problems and sins that must be addressed. In Greek, the word "saint" is *hagios,* which is the same word as 'holy,' or 'set apart,' or 'sanctified.' All those translations come from the same word. Regardless of behavior, Paul called the Christians the "saints" of God – the sanctified holy ones of God. He can do that because he is speaking of eternal realities instead of present conditions. He said, "I no longer regard anyone after the flesh ...if any one is in Christ, he is a brand new creation!"[21] Paul is seeing the people through Christ's eyes. He is seeing their character being washed and sanctified through Christ. He is seeing them reborn in Spirit, made after the image and likeness of God. He sees that the Corinthians are indeed *holy* in spite of themselves!

The Corinthian Heresy

Because Paul taught the righteousness of Christ, and not human attempts to live by a moral code of conduct, he was accused of preaching lawlessness by the legalists who came to oppose his ministry everywhere he went. The Corinthian letters reveal one misinterpretation of Paul's message. It is known as *the Corinthian heresy*. The Corinthians had a background in Greek philosophy, which tended to divide the human being into two parts: the soul (or mind) and the body. In some circles, the mind with its capacity for reason was completely good, but the body was evil and full of passions. This philosophy came to be called *dualism*. When Paul preached salvation, these Greeks thought that the soul was saved, but it did not matter what you did in the body because the body was evil and was perishing anyway. They thought that since they were "sanctified" in their souls, they could live any way they wanted to in the body – even engaging in immorality.

You can just see Paul holding his head in his hands when he hears about some of the immorality promoted in Corinth in the name of Jesus! You can see him just shaking his head and saying to himself, "How could this be?" The message of faith is so hard for the natural mind to grasp that immorality is a "natural" consequence of human misunderstanding. So, years after he has been in Corinth, including the two or three years he spent building the church there, he now has to go back and explain in a letter that "No, just because you are sanctified doesn't mean you can continue in immorality." I am sure he was disheartened at the inability of their natural minds

---

[21] 2 Cor. 5:16 – 17

to grasp the truth of the message he preached. It was a message that can only be grasped by faith and by the Spirit. The human counterfeit will always be legalism or lawlessness. It is no wonder Paul received such opposition from Jewish believers wherever he went.

Paul was accused of preaching the same sort of lawlessness in other areas including Galatia and Rome. "And why not do evil that good may come? – as some people slanderously charge us with saying …"[22] This was a possible misinterpretation of his message, but not at all what he was preaching. Paul expected to see people who were transformed by Christ and who turned away from evil deeds, but he also knew that the only way to produce a lasting change in our character is by faith. Paul knew that when we receive God's righteousness by faith, the inevitable result is a transformed life. However, Paul wanted to put the righteousness of God in us in its proper perspective. Righteousness is a *result* of our fellowship with God, not *a condition* for fellowship. He said, "If you are walking by the Spirit, *then you will not fulfill the desires of the flesh.*"[23] It is impossible to walk in sin, which is bondage to compulsive behavior, and to walk in faith at the same time, because faith produces the liberty of the Spirit, which *is* freedom from sin. So, if you are walking by faith, you will not sin.

Faith and sin are incompatible realities, just as light and darkness cannot be joined. If you are enslaved to any sin, to the degree you are enslaved, you are not walking in faith.[24] Faith in Jesus will set you free. It will set you free not only from the consequence of sin but from participation in it as well. Faith has power to break the bondage of sin in our lives. *Good intentions will produce remorse and even short-term changes in our actions, but we will not be permanently changed by guilt, condemnation, or fear.* We all do many things we know are wrong, but that does not give us the power to stop doing it. Even when we control our outward behavior by sheer force of will and do not act upon our lusts for a season, we still cannot stop the thoughts of our hearts nor turn them from lust to holiness. And yet, that is the tragedy of religious

---

[22] Romans 3: 8
[23] Galatians 5:16
[24] Romans 6

legalism. It tries to achieve righteousness through good behavior when only God can produce it inside us by his Spirit.[25] That is why Jesus said, "Everyone who commits sin is a slave to sin, ...but if the Son of Man sets you free, you will be free indeed."[26]

Sanctification: Being Free From the Desire to Sin

Jesus is offering us a righteousness that not only changes our behavior, but also changes the inward desires of our hearts. For example, who is more free from the addiction of smoking, the man who quit smoking but still wants a cigarette or the man who never smoked in the first place? Why, the second of course, because he is not even tempted! Jesus promises us the second kind of liberty –not just outward reform but inward transformation of desire– so that sin is not even a temptation to us! *That is true freedom.* That is the power of true faith at work in us. *Religion may teach us to restrain our outward behavior, but only God can take away our desire to sin.* God's cleansing of our desires is the power of sanctification at work in our lives. God's power is released into our lives through Jesus as we turn to him and away from the poverty of ourselves. In fact, God's desire is to stop us from trying to perfect ourselves so that we might rely upon him more fully. All we can do is confess that we are sinful; it's God's job to "forgive our sins and cleanse us from all unrighteousness," (I John 1:9). The burden stops here.

Faith is Obedience

So, you cannot separate faith in God from the fruit of sanctification. True faith *will* produce holy living. If you really understand what Jesus has done for you on the cross, it will break the yoke of your bondage to sin, and you will walk free of its power. Doubt will cause you to remain in bondage, because you doubt both God's willingness and ability to set you free. You doubt his love and his favor towards you. You doubt his acceptance of you. As a result, you will have an uneasy conscience, and you will struggle to attain peace with God through some effort of your own. You will trust yourself and not Jesus.

---

[25] Romans 8:1 – 4
[26] John 8: 34–36

The writer of Hebrews uses a word meaning "no faith" when he describes disobedience in the children of Israel, (Hebrews 4: 6). The word is *a-peitho*, or no trust, *(a = no; peitho = trust)*. The word, *peitho*, in Greek means to "trust in, rely upon, and act upon the word of one's superior." The idea is that willing submission to a spoken word by a superior will issue forth in obedience. If one distrusts that word, then one does not act upon it. Therefore, faith's natural consequence is obedience, while unbelief issues forth in disobedience. Faith = obedience; unbelief = sin. The example from Exodus that is referred to by the writer of Hebrews shows how unbelief causes sin: Israel failed to enter into the promised land when Joshua and Caleb returned with a good report because *the people did not believe* what God had already spoken to them about Canaan. They believed the bad report instead, so they disobeyed God's desire for them. They failed to enter in to the purposes of God for their lives because of unbelief. They missed the reward God had for them and they died in the wilderness.[27]

Again, Paul is saying in Galatians, that if we really believe what God has done for us on the cross, we *will* walk free of sin! We *will* obey. *We will walk in the promised land of sanctification, God's Sabbath rest.* We will cease our striving to overcome sin. We will let the power of God destroy our prison doors. We will walk free from the power of sin! Faith in God, combined with his power, is incompatible with sin. Our obedience in faith will crush sin beneath our feet. Sin will lose its power over us, as we believe in God.

Unbelief is Sin

The other side of the coin is this: if we do not believe what God has done for us on the cross, then we will fall into disobedience. Although this is a strong statement, all unbelief leads us to certain types of actions. Those actions are all based upon a mistrust of God, so they cannot be pleasing to God. Before Eve sinned, before she ate the forbidden fruit in the Garden of Eden, she doubted God's truthfulness. Her action of disobedience was the result of her disbelief. Unbelief is sin because it leads to actions motivated by

---

[27] Hebrews 3:17– 4:11

a lack of trust in God. When God says Jesus has already sanctified us and has given us his righteousness as a free gift, and we act as if these things are not true, we are doubting God and the actions that follow spring from our unbelief. These actions cannot be pleasing to God. So, there is a consequence if we neglect the perfect sufficiency of Jesus. We fall back to self-trust, we lose our peace with God, and self-trust produces in us agitation, despair, jealousy, intolerance, meanness, and it eventually leads to overt sins, like sexual immorality, theft, and murder.

What is happening to us? We are trying to bring an unacceptable sacrifice to God. We are trying to offer God our own righteousness, and God has said our righteousness is not acceptable to him. When we offer an unacceptable sacrifice, we can feel God's rejection of that sacrifice, and it leads to a lack of peace. We are striving in our flesh to find peace with God, and instead of peace, we find guilt and shame. The cycle continues because our fear and guilt then cause us to try and make up for our failings. Like a man on parole, we try to live a better life and be a better "Christian." We want to offer our new obedience a sacrifice for sin, as if we could be worthy enough to make a perfect sacrifice. To our dismay, instead of finding peace, we are *still* left with our guilt and fear.

Since Jesus made that sacrifice for us, there is "no longer any sacrifice for sin,"[28] and our efforts, as another sacrifice, cannot produce peace with God. Even though God has already given us his peace, we are not trusting Christ's sacrifice for us. *Because we are not believing God,* we neglect his peace and try to please God through our own efforts. As the cycle continues, and as our own efforts fail to produce peace, we fall into despair about our relationship to God, and our despair produces either legalistic religion or sensual abandon.

As you can see, the cycle of unbelief produces these sins. To escape the cycle of unbelief and sin, we must believe God's word to us that Jesus is our sacrifice for sin, our righteousness, *and* our sanctification.[29]

---

[28] Hebrew 10:18
[29] 1 Corinthians 1:30

Already and Not Yet

Clearly, there is a difference between the reality of Christ's sacrifice on the cross and the expression of Christ's perfect character in our personality. Yes, there is a process whereby that sanctification is made visible in us. Paul recognized the limitations of our humanity. He recognized that our appropriation of the benefits of Jesus would take time. Because of our frailty and ignorance, we will not grasp all that Jesus has done for us in a single day, yet our lack of understanding does not change the Truth. We will grow in the knowledge of the Lord's redeeming power as we enter into a relationship with him. As we seek his presence and intimacy with him, we will become like him.

Approaching God Honestly

Probably, one of the most important aspects of our faith is to know that Jesus accepts us just as we are. We can come to him easily, no matter how badly damaged we are, as long as we come to him honestly. His grace should allow us to freely admit our failures, faults, and sins. We need not pretend to be perfect, or to be better than we are. We can come to him, confessing openly our weakness. In that attitude of honesty, we can freely approach our God. The truth is: if we abide in Jesus, and his word abides in us, then we will bear fruit through our relationship with him.[30] Paul says that holy character is a fruit of abiding in relationship with God by the Holy Spirit:

> *By contrast, the fruit of the Spirit is love, joy, peace, patience, kindness, generosity, faith, gentleness, and self-control. There is no law against such things. –Galatians 5:22-23*

---

[30] "I am the true vine, and my Father is the gardener. He cuts off every branch in me that bears no fruit, while every branch that does bear fruit he prunes so that it will be even more fruitful. You are already clean because of the word I have spoken to you. Remain in me, and I will remain in you. No branch can bear fruit by itself; it must remain in the vine. Neither can you bear fruit unless you remain in me. "I am the vine; you are the branches. If a man remains in me and I in him, he will bear much fruit; apart from me you can do nothing. If anyone does not remain in me, he is like a branch that is thrown away and withers; such branches are picked up, thrown into the fire and burned. If you remain in me and my words remain in you, ask whatever you wish, and it will be given you. This is to my Father's glory, that you bear much fruit, showing yourselves to be my disciples. (John 15:1–8, NIV)

Paul calls the character of righteousness a fruit of the Holy Spirit!!! [31] What a simple equation! If we want righteousness, the only way that righteousness will form itself in us is if we abide in fellowship with the Lord. Deeds will flow out of that relationship. Even faith is one of the fruits of that relationship. *So, intimacy with Jesus produces greater faith.* None of these things is gained by our labors; all flow out of our trust in Jesus. Again, I am saying to you, sanctification is the result of our relationship with Jesus, not the means to enter into his presence.

Truth is an Experience Not Just an Idea

The knowledge of the truth of sanctification is like preparing a nursery for a new baby. It isn't the baby, but it is a place prepared for the baby when the baby finally arrives. The baby in this case is knowing Jesus as your Sanctifier in a very personal way. I've stretched you intellectually and theologically with the truth of who you are in Christ, but it must be more than that. You must be able to experience the Love of God for yourself and it must heal you of your fears, otherwise it isn't a reality in your life; it's just an idea. In later chapters, I'm going to address blocks to faith and healing, because there is more to it than just knowing in your head that God has sanctified you. But by teaching the truth, we can clear away many false ideas, which prevent you from accepting what Jesus has done for you. Being established in the truth of what Jesus has done for you on the cross is the first step in laying hold of the power of his sanctification of you. Knowing what Jesus has done for you is part of the excitement of preparation, so that you can enjoy the fulfillment of it when it comes. More on this subject later … ❦

---

[31] Galatians 5:22–23 provide a list of attributes which describe a righteous character.

Chapter Four

Sanctification: a Practical Application

Sanctify them through thy truth: thy word is truth.
—John 17:17

Let's apply the principle of sanctification by faith to a common problem. Most of my life I struggled with the problem of lust of the eyes. Whether it was a pretty girl or a nice painting, my attention could be transfixed by the object of beauty. You and I both know that there is no holiness in the lust of the eyes, for soon the imagination – or the Tempter – will place a thought in my mind that does not belong there.

Though I knew I was guilty, there was not a thing I could do about it. I was and am happily married and content with my beautiful wife; yet, my eyes could lead me astray! Why? Who knows? But one thing I found out, the more I got mad at myself and the more I resisted the practice and condemned myself, the more I would find myself unable to break free of the habit. When I thought I had conquered it, it would soon creep back in and surprise me by showing itself in some way I had not expected.

Repression and restraint of desire is not the same thing as being free from desire. A guilty conscience may cause us to repress our impulses or restrain our actions, but it cannot remove the desire from within our hearts. Like pushing down with your hand on a stick of soft butter, the butter will squeeze out through your fingers and out the sides of your hand, no matter how hard you try to keep it contained. So too, lusts and desires cannot be contained simply by keeping a tight lid on them.

If the truth be told, you have struggled or are still struggling in the same way; perhaps not over this particular sin or temptation, but with another temptation peculiar to your weakness and personality. In Romans 7, Paul talks about this inescapable nature of sin manifesting itself in the flesh. When the Law of God reveals sin in our lives, whether that be in our thoughts or our deeds, knowledge of the Law produces guilt in our conscience, but it does not change our behavior: we know what's right but cannot do it; we don't want to do what's wrong, but we do it anyway (vs. 15-20). Simply having the *knowledge* of what is right does not give us the power to do what is right!

Now my first reaction to the impulse of some lust in myself was to deny it, repress it, and try to get control of it and stop its working in me. I might try fasting and praying (neither of which worked!) or I might try to control my outward behavior by forcing my eyes away. But no matter what I did, the pull of that temptation kept coming back and dragging me to stare unconsciously! What a mess! And what an evil, deceived person I am, thinking somehow I was or could be righteous in myself! No, I am certainly not my own savior. *I am the problem, not the solution.*

My failure to cure myself led me to another course of action. My next step was to get brutally honest with God. "This is what I am God; this is what I do. I know I shouldn't, but I can't seem to change it or help myself. So, I am confessing to you that I need you. I need you to save me from myself. I can't do it." When I began to do that, grace entered in. And although I did not overcome the habit, grace allowed me to face the problem and confess it openly to God without the fear of being rejected or condemned by him. Then I found the power of the unrighteous desire beginning to wane in me.

Conversely, when we repress, deny, or condemn ourselves for our sins and failures, it only makes the sin more powerful.[32] The same thing happens when we try to mentally control our

---

[32] Paul speaks of this psychology of temptation, sin, and knowledge of the law in Romans 7:5-13. Paul shows how conscience increases the power of temptation. As a child, perhaps, he was not so tempted, but as soon as he learned some things were wrong and he shouldn't do them, he was overwhelmed with a desire for what was forbidden: "I was once alive apart from the law, but when the commandment came, sin came alive and I died; but sin, finding opportunity in the commandment, created in me all kinds of covetousness. Apart from the law sin lies dead."

behavior through sheer force of will. Outward restraint increases inner desire! This increase of the power of temptation taught me something about the deception of trying to be a good Christian. I was so afraid of being evil and trying so hard to be good that I did not rely on Jesus to set me free or be my strength. It was *me* trying to conquer sin in *my* life through *my* strength. *I* am the problem and yet *I* am trying to be the solution. *I was trying to be my own savior!* Like a person trying to pull himself out of quicksand: the harder I struggled, the deeper I sank in sin. I needed someone on the outside of the pit to throw me a rope and pull me out. That person was Jesus.

When we are tempted by sin in this way, we are often driven by fear and guilt from the presence of Christ. In a perverse way, the fear keeps us bound to temptation and sin. Fear of condemnation, of failure, and of being weak, causes us to turn away from our Savior and turn to ourselves. Fear causes us to try to save ourselves from sin through good works. It doesn't succeed, but we try anyway. Because we know we shouldn't be a certain way or do a certain thing, our conscience bothers us. Because our conscience bothers us, we try to escape the power of sin, but we end up trying to escape from God as well. Like Adam in the Garden, who hid from God because of his sin, we too want to hide from God when we know we are wrong. Fear drives us from God, and so we are separated from the only One who could help us escape the power of sin!

The Necessity of Confession

There is a remedy for this cycle of fear and sin. It is called confession. Confession forces us to be honest with God about our weakness in the face of habitual sin, and confession breaks the power of sin over us. Honesty before God removes our fear and our feelings of condemnation. Confession removes sin's power of control over us; dishonesty causes that power to return.

One of the most common responses of a troubled conscience is to deny the reality of sin. We deny that we have done anything wrong. Like Adam in the Garden, it is not our fault! However, our denials do not work to heal us. God's remedy for a troubled conscience is open confession:

> This is the message we have heard from him and proclaim to you, that God is light and in him there is no darkness at all. If we say that we have fellowship with him while we are walking in darkness, we lie and do not do what is true; but if we walk in the light as he himself is in the light, we have fellowship with one another, and the blood of Jesus his Son cleanses us from all sin. If we say that we have no sin, we deceive ourselves, and the truth is not in us. If we confess our sins, he who is faithful and just will forgive us our sins and cleanse us from all unrighteousness. If we say that we have not sinned, we make him a liar, and his word is not in us. —1 John 1:5-10, NRSV

Confession brings the gift of freedom from self-condemnation. When we are honest with God about our faults, we no longer condemn ourselves and fear gradually loses its power over us. We are set free to worship and to obey.

Confession of sin, and faith in God's power to heal me, changed my struggle with temptation to victory. I realized the deception that Satan was throwing my way. He was telling me that if I just tried hard enough, I could beat this thing and then everything would be okay with God. He was throwing me back upon myself. I was falling for that old lie that my works = my righteousness. I was forgetting Christ and striving in myself, but as I began to understand that Jesus Christ is my sanctification, I began to apply faith to this seemingly intractable problem. I finally began to *believe* that *God* could heal me of this sin! And I began to believe that now, empowered by the Holy Spirit, I could overcome these sins by *his* strength at work in me. Rather than striving in my flesh to be righteous, I began to walk by the Spirit and began to trust Christ *to be* my righteousness. So, as I let his righteousness pour into me, his righteousness washed away my uncleanness like a flood.

Transforming the Mind

Paul says we are to take every thought captive to make even our thoughts obey the truth of Christ![33] How hard, even impossible, it is for a person to do if they are not operating in faith! It becomes just another fruitless work of the flesh because you start arguing with your own mind, and you end up losing! But with faith, I found that the "just requirement of the law can be fulfilled in us, who walk not in the strength of our flesh, but in the power of the Holy Spirit."[34] By a growing confidence of the power of Jesus Christ at work in me, which is faith, I began to take captive the thoughts which tempted me to try to perfect myself and to make myself righteous! *I didn't come against the first temptation, the lust of the eyes, which was obvious, but the second!* I came against the desire of my flesh to make myself good (like that old man out on parole), and I confessed "there is no good thing in me."[35] I repented of myself. Then I turned to Jesus and believed his Word. I said, "You are my righteousness and my sanctification," and I stopped trying to perfect myself through my strength.

Now armed with faith in Jesus and the knowledge that his blood covered my sins, I said to that thought of lust, "I am sanctified (cleansed and healed) of you already by what Jesus has already done for me on the cross. Jesus is my righteousness and he is my sanctification. I don't have to struggle with you or over you because you are already defeated by his blood. And I am victorious over you." The cycle – of fear, guilt, denial, self-perfection, failure and condemnation – was broken in me by the knowledge God had given me, and sin started to lose its power.

Now, what I am saying may not have much effect upon you and you may have a hard time grasping it with your reasoning mind, but I was speaking to that sin out of revelation of who Jesus is and what he has already done for me. I know what Jesus has done for me. This isn't some mind game. This is an example of dealing with

---

[33] 2 Corinthians 10:5
[34] Romans 8:4
[35] Romans 7:18

a problem of temptation through maturity in faith. It may not be as simple for you until you really understand what it means to have Jesus as your sanctifier. I can only tell you what standing on the Rock of revelation has done for me in my struggle against sin: that old temptation just curled up, shriveled, and died!

Now Satan continues to be a tempter, and he brings that thought back from time to time, but now each time he does, instead of feeling condemned, I take authority over that thought pattern and take it captive and break its power. I tell Satan, "I don't have to be perfect, good, or righteous; Jesus did that for me. So don't try to condemn me for being what I am, Jesus paid the price for that too. Now because *he* is righteous and has paid the price to set me free from sin, I will not fall to your temptations. Get out of my face!" To me, after years of struggle, that sin is finally a defeated enemy! And I am standing in the victory that Jesus died to give me. It says in first John, Jesus came to destroy the works of the Evil One, not just cleanse us after we fall.[36] The power of his sanctification does more than just forgive us; it removes the manifestation of sin, both in attitude *and* in deeds.

Sanctified in the Truth

Jesus prayed that we would be sanctified in, or by, the truth.[37] It is God's truth which completes the work of sanctification in us. Knowing the truth of what Jesus *has already done for us* sets us free! Our trust in his finished work frees us from the power of sin. Our trust in the power of the cross breaks the bondage of sin. Because it is necessary to trust Christ to become free, it is the reason *faith is the one work that God requires of us*.[38] For if we do not believe that Jesus has already done what is necessary , we will be thrown back upon ourselves to struggle against sin in the inadequate power of our flesh. That is why faith is essential and mandatory on our part. *It is the obedience* that God requires.

Though I do not believe in works that produce righteousness,

---

[36] 1 John 3:8

[37] John 17:17

[38] Jesus answered and said unto them, This is the work of God, that you believe in him whom he has sent." (John 6:29) "But without faith it is impossible to please God: for he that comes to God must believe that he is, and that he is a rewarder of those who diligently seek him." (Hebrews 11:6)

faith is the one work that God requires of us because without faith we cannot stand in the truth of his saving power. By faith, we come to know God more intimately. We come to know him as he works through love to set us free. Our faith in him allows us to be set free from fretful striving. By standing in faith, we are then able enter into the Rest of his love.[39] And what does he ask us to believe? He calls us to believe that we have *already* been made righteous and that we have *already* been sanctified by Jesus' death on the cross! He calls us to rest in the knowledge that no more work is required of us except to believe in what he has done. *He is calling us to believe that he has done for us what we could not do for ourselves.* Give praise to God, people!

The Snare of Unbelief and the Spirit of Manipulation

When we do not believe his Word, when we do not respond to God in faith, we inevitably fall back into the bondage of some sin and into the deception of legalism. Unbelief automatically throws us back into the striving of our flesh. Our eyes are taken off Christ, our Savior, and are put back upon ourselves – our labors and our efforts. Then we are "cut off from Christ" and have fallen away from grace.[40] That does not mean we lose our salvation. Paul is just describing the practical reality of being thrown again into the bondage of being our own saviors. We don't lose our salvation, we don't even lose our sanctification, but we forget what Christ died for and we start worshiping at the altar of our own ability to be religious and good. Paul says, when we do look to ourselves, we are not in faith. There is "nothing good" in us, as Paul says, and so, we cannot find any ground to stand on by looking to our own good deeds. It is hopeless to look within for a righteousness that will satisfy either God or conscience. There is no faith in that! However, since faith in Jesus is obedience to God, *then faith is righteousness.*[41] No religious behavior or good deeds are righteousness. No restraint of sin is righteousness. Faith is the

---

[39] Isaiah 26: 3 Thou wilt keep him in perfect peace, whose mind is stayed on thee: because he trusteth in thee. (Isaiah 26:3, KJV)

[40] Galatians 5:4

[41] For in it the righteousness of God is revealed through faith for faith; as it is written, "He who is righteous through faith shall live." (Romans 1:17, RSV – see also Romans 4)

only righteousness that God respects and requires. It is the only thing in us he "counts" as righteous.

If believing in and trusting Christ is our sole righteousness, then we need to be aware of all counterfeit claims of obedience to Christ. One common counterfeit claim is a call to religious activity. It can take the form of the most innocent coercion, like the call to attend Wednesday night prayer meetings. If not done in the right spirit, such a call to religious observance can be a manipulation that strikes like a dagger at the heart of Christian freedom. As a pastor, I write to you pastors to beware of making use of some veiled implication that "If you don't attend such and such a meeting, then you are missing God!" What a murderous misuse of the call of God! It is using guilt to manipulate the flock instead of using faith to appeal to their faith.

One of my favorite passages from scripture warns about the subtlety of religious counterfeits:

> *Why do you submit to regulations like, "Do not handle, Do not taste, Do not touch" because of some human traditions and doctrines. These things indeed have an appearance of wisdom in promoting rigor of devotion and self-abasement and severity to the body, but they are of no value, serving only to indulge the flesh. –Colossians 2:20-23 (alternate NIV translation)*

I've heard many teachers say things like, "Yes brother, if you only FAST and PRAY, God will be happy with you and your prayers will be answered!" What a deception! Yes, there is a time for fasting …if it is done in faith. But you can fast until you are skin and bones, and it won't do you any good at all – except to make you proud and religiously arrogant. You will think you are pleasing God, when all you are doing is exalting yourself! That is not faith; that is flesh!

Beware of the subtle spirit of manipulation: that witchcraft that looks like righteousness but ensnares the soul. You can counterfeit faith with religious exercise. You can go to every meeting the church has; you can pray for hours on end, you can tithe and give offerings, and you may look good to all the church; you can even be an elder or a deacon, but you can also be entertaining the spirit of death.

I have seen many congregations ensnared by the manipulation of guilt. Manipulation produces "righteous living" for a short time, and then it becomes so burdensome that even the faithful begin to look for excuses not to follow the pastor, the board, or the priest. Watch out for words like: "You have to do this; you need to do this; you have to; you need to; you better; you must ...or we need to, we must, we ought..." All these phrases are followed by an implied "or else." Jesus never used those phrases. He just said things like, "Watch and pray, Come follow me, Go and do thou likewise!" He always spoke faith to the hearer, and then he *always* left his hearer free to choose how to respond. He didn't add to his command some manipulative trick. He left the person with only two choices: obedience or disobedience, but he never robbed them of their dignity in the process. He respected the integrity of their choices, even if they made the wrong ones. He never denied their freedom; he honored them for the image of God in them. He never used people to further some goal, like building a church, because for Jesus, people are the goal.

For me, it has always been pretty easy to tell when I am being manipulated by guilt, whether it is an appeal to give money or to spend more time in church meetings in order to be a good Christian. Somehow, somewhere, in my gut, the preaching or the teaching causes me anxiety and to break out in a sweat of fear that I am not living up to what God expects of me. I'm told, to correct that situation, I only need to jump through one more hoop ...like increase my giving or attend one more meeting or pray a little bit more. Yet, even when I do jump through the hoop, my mind says, "You still haven't done enough; you should be doing even more." There is no end to this line of thought because the truth is no matter how much we do, it will never be enough to fulfill all the righteousness that a holy and perfect God requires. Faith alone brings us to the place of acknowledgement of our poverty. Faith alone causes us to see our good works as "filthy rags." Faith alone causes us to see that our *only hope* for righteousness in this life is Jesus. And faith causes us to surrender our foolish attempts to make ourselves like Jesus. Faith alone is our righteousness.

Paul's great confession in Romans is that the Gospel of God is the power of God to bring salvation. In that Gospel, he declares that faith is the same thing as righteousness: "He who through faith is righteous shall live!"[42] If we want God's righteousness, it is received by believing in him. ҉

---

[42] For I am not ashamed of the gospel: it is the power of God for salvation to every one who has faith, to the Jew first and also to the Greek. For in it the righteousness of God is revealed through faith for faith; as it is written, "He who through faith is righteous shall live." (Romans 1: 16–18, RSV)

Chapter Five

Laboring to Rest: The Contrary Nature of Human Striving

Therefore, while the promise of entering his rest remains, let us fear lest any of you be judged to have failed to reach it. For good news came to us just as to them; but the message which they heard did not benefit them, because it did not meet with faith in the hearers. For we who have believed enter that rest ...So then, there remains a sabbath rest for the people of God; for whoever enters God's rest also ceases from his labors as God did from his. Let us therefore strive to enter that rest, that no one fall by the same sort of disobedience (unbelief).
–Hebrews 4:1-3, 9-11, RSV

"Let us labor to enter that rest ..." What a paradox to be told that we must strive to enter the Lord's rest! Yet, in Hebrews, it says we enter the Lord's rest by the labor of believing! Faith allows us the privilege of entering the rest of God. I do not know of any area where I have struggled more than this: in renewing my mind to the truth of God's perfect work for me in Jesus. My mind and my flesh rebel against this knowledge of God. In my natural state, faith makes no sense to me. "How do I believe? How do I have faith?" My soul cries out, "Give me a nice and easy two-step process. Teach me the ABC's of believing."

But faith does not come by a formula. God is so jealous for you that he will not allow you to learn faith by some impersonal process. You will not be able to go to some other human being to get faith. Faith comes only one way: by intimacy with the One who created you. He will not let your soul rest until you come to him. God is so intensely personal, and cares so much for you as an individual, that he has created only one way for you to come to maturity: through fellowship with him. If you want to get faith from a book, forget it. All the book can do is to point you to the Author and Finisher of your faith, but the words on the page won't give you faith ...at least not without encountering the Holy Spirit in the Word on the page. If you want to be established in your faith, go to the One who created you, and find him. Learn what he is like.

Now that sounds like a contradiction. I told you a little while ago I hate pietism with all its recommendations for having a quiet time and reading the bible. Yet now, it appears I am saying that very thing! Or am I? Look, to break you of your legalistic thinking, you have to be shocked out of your expectations. My objection to quiet times is not based upon an objection to spending time with Jesus. My objection is putting quiet time into a law book of "good" Christian behavior and putting God on a time clock: here I go with my one hour of quiet time every morning ...I punch in my time card and I spend my minutes with God ...Doesn't that sound ridiculous? Would you do that with your earthly parent? Would you put your relationship to your earthly father on a time card, "Okay, Dad, you have an hour of my time"? What an offense that would be to a parent who loves you! If you did that with your parent to fulfill an obligation for relationship, wouldn't you agree that your relationship is in deep trouble – or at least has some severe problems? Why then would you do that with God? Why would you put your friendship with him on a clock? What does that tell you about your relationship with him? That in order to be his friend, you have to treat him like a boss who measures every minute of your behavior with a punch card? That is not faith; that is religion!

Faith Through Relationship

Faith is something that is built out of a friendship with God. Faith comes from knowing God's love for you. It is built through a relationship; and relationships, by their very nature, require time spent together. They grow intimate through shared time. Faith is a natural byproduct of that relationship, just like breathing is part of living. Jesus said, "I am the vine, you are the branches. If a man abides in me and I in him, he will bear much fruit," (John 15: 5). Fruit is the evidence of a relationship with Jesus. It is the product of that living friendship. Paul talked about the fruit of character that comes from the lifestyle of being in the presence of God. He called this fruit the evidence of God's character in us: "But the fruit of the Spirit is love, joy, peace, long suffering, kindness, goodness, *faith,* gentleness, and self-control," (Galatians 5:22-23). Look how we learn faith! Faith is one of the elements of character developed from a Spirit-filled walk while abiding in relationship with Jesus.

Growing in faith is not some super-spiritual hocus-pocus. It is not some mysterious work on our part. It is God's mysterious work in us! He is molding and shaping us so that we will trust and believe in him. It takes time, but God's goal is to make us like his Son Jesus, who trusts and believes the Father. Faith is rather simple, really. Faith has been given to you if you believe in Jesus Christ. The Holy Spirit, who lives within you, already believes the Father, and his faith is working within you to make you a servant of faith. God is working to remove deceptions from your life, which block faith's operation. If you desire Jesus more than power; if you desire him more than position or prestige; if your desire to be his friend is greater than your need for recognition; *then* faith will begin to flow out of you as naturally as water flows downstream. Why? Because out of the relationship you are developing with the Lord, you will be healed and faith will arise within your spirit. Faith will grow in you as naturally as the warm summer sun causes the flowers to bloom.

If you seek Jesus, you will find him. There is no law that you have to seek him. You do not have to pursue him, but if you want to be established in faith, then there appears to be no substitute for abiding in him. If your desire is strong enough, then you will pursue intimacy.

Past Rejection, Failure, and Love

Most of us, at one time or another, have feared to expose ourselves to God. We have been afraid to be intimate with him because we are afraid that our sins and misdeeds were so terrible and our failures so great that God would not accept us. This false understanding of our Father destroys our hope and faith. Our Father wants us to learn a lesson more essential to our well-being than success and sinlessness: *he wants us to know that it is okay to have failed.* It is okay to be weak. It is okay to have failed in your battle against sin. *You need to know that. You need to know you are already accepted by him, not because of your perfect behavior, but because of his great love for you.* You need to know his mercy and grace towards you because it will give you the courage to walk with him. You need to be able to rest in the knowledge that the *only* righteousness you have is through Jesus.

It is still a struggle to abide in the truth of our acceptance in Christ. Our emotions fight against our intellect. Our past experiences of rejection become more powerful to us than any abstract talk about God's great love for us. So much of that kind of talk seems like an unreality. We know we are loved because of God's Word, but we still feel like God is a million miles from our heart. If we could just experience the love of God, then maybe we could be comfortable in his presence.

Views of Human Nature: the Battle of Intellect and Emotions and Faith

I used to battle depression and discouragement all the time in my relationship with God. I used to feel like I could never be "good enough" to be pleasing to God. I was so conscious of my shortcomings. I could not see anything but my own weakness. I could not believe. I could not hope. I certainly had no faith, and I doubted God's ability to deliver me from my situation. Finally, I found out a strategy for battle that could turn my situation around. *I stopped letting my emotions be my god.* There *is* a labor involved in entering God's rest: it is bringing our thoughts and emotions into subjection to the Word of God. This process is vital, but so little understood by the Church, that I want to relate in some detail what it means to labor for the presence of God. Most of this labor takes place in the mind, the will, and the emotions, or the human soul. The soul, however, is only one aspect of human nature, and if we do not bring to bear the power of the Spirit on our human nature, we are bound to live defeated lives.

So many people understand human nature from a Greek perspective that the biblical understanding of human nature is lost to our culture. It is even lost to our seminaries and to much of the mainline church. I studied for three years in seminary and never got a clear picture of how God made us. We need to understand how we are made in order to know how we can be healed.

Let me diagram for you the difference between a Greek and a biblical view of Human Nature:

Biblical (Hebrew) Model

Greek Model

Spirit

Soul-Reason → Soul → Mind: Intellect, Reason & Thoughts
→ Emotions: Feelings, etc.
→ Will: Decision Making, Choices, etc.

Body   Body

Greek and Biblical Views of Human Nature

The ancient Greek culture understood the nature of a human being to be of two parts: an eternal *soul* and a mortal *body*. The human mind of reason was the main characteristic of the soul, and it was "good." They believed that the thoughts or ideas of the mind were pure. Reason was the ideal characteristic in a human being. As long as a man's reasoning was accurate, then he lived in the truth and was a good person. Against this ideal nature, humanity had two enemies: ignorance and the passions of the body expressed through appetites and lusts. The Greeks thought that if a person could just understand with his mind the true nature of reality, he could *then* rule over the desires and passions of his body through the use of his reason. If he had both knowledge and control of his body, he would then be a good or ideal person.

Most of western culture still operates with this Greek picture of humanity, and it is taught in our public schools in the United States. That is why there is so much stress on education in our society. We think that if we just teach people what is right, they will do it. We believe that through education, prejudice, racism, drugs, and unwanted pregnancies will just disappear. However, hatred, prejudice, and fear are powers in the human personality that defy reason and logic. They are much stronger than knowledge. They run through the tapestry of the human soul and are as deeply embedded in the human personality as is the desire for life and breath.

A second problem with the Greek model is that the Greeks did not understand that the human mind *itself* is corrupted by the power of sin. The mind is not entirely innocent and pure or ideal as the Greeks supposed. The mind can be used to actively resist the knowledge of God. We might not even know we are resisting God with our minds, because there can be a logic to unbelief and to atheism. When this happens, reason itself is a source of deception rather than a source of truth. If you have ever met people who are full of hatred towards a race or group of people, you know they all can give you many *reasons* why they believe the way they do. There can be a logic to hatred and prejudice. The Nazis in Germany clearly demonstrated the use of logic to justify their belief in a Master Race and to persecute people who, in their eyes, were "sub-human" and "dysgenic."

In less dramatic ways, reason and logic can be used to provide excuses for selfish or greedy behavior. People used the Bible to justify slavery before the Civil War. People offer many reasons to excuse themselves when they cheat on taxes, tell white lies, or steal office supplies from work. We can make many excuses for failing to give offerings to God or alms to the poor. It is so easy to blind ourselves to other people's needs by reasoning about our own. Reason can even blind us to the truth about our relationship to God. Reason is powerless to redeem society. Reason by itself is not capable of reforming human character or producing righteousness. Reason, unredeemed by the Spirit of God, does nothing to lead us to the truth.

The Consequence of Greek Thinking

In the Church in the West, we have fallen prey to this Greek model of understanding humanity. In subtle ways, we have substituted our knowledge *about* God for his call to intimacy *with* him. Our theology has become an excuse for our lack of relationship. We know the words on the page, but we don't know the One who wrote the book! Because of our desire for abstract knowledge about God, our churches mimic the Greek model of education. We are concerned almost entirely with the intellect and with the communication of ideas, while we neglect the *practice* of the faith. As a result, instead of producing disciples of Jesus, we create students who are more concerned with doctrinal purity *(having the correct ideas)* than in living the life of Christ in a fallen world. For example, it is much easier to memorize the verse "love your enemies" than it is to actually put it into practice. In that simple command of God, we see the difference between the Greek and the biblical goals of education. The first requires only mental understanding; the second requires a way of life.

The Biblical Model

Because the Greeks divided humanity into two parts (the idealized soul and the passionate appetites of the flesh), they sought to reform character simply by imparting information to the intellect. The Hebrews saw a unity of the whole person (*body, mind* and *spirit*), in which each aspect plays a part in human motivation.

The Hebrew model of education is entirely different than the Greek. The Hebrew method is visceral and dynamic and is best illustrated by Jesus' actions as he trained the disciples. He had them learn as they went along with him. They watched him lay hands on the sick and heal those with diseases, and then he had the disciples do the same. He explained to them what he was doing, and why, as they walked along with him. Then he showed them how to do it. Finally, he sent them out to teach others.[43]

Jesus took this model of education from God's instructions to the children of Israel. God instructed parents to teach their children the words of God, not in a classroom, but as part of the everyday course of life.

Fix these words of mine in your hearts and minds; tie them as symbols on your hands and bind them on your foreheads. Teach them to your children, talking about them when you sit at home and when you walk along the road, when you lie down and when you get up. –Deuteronomy 11:18-19, NIV

Life became the classroom and the children learned by seeing, asking, and doing. This model of instruction makes it easy to apply the knowledge a person gains to all of life. Also, the example of those who teach becomes part of the educational process. The character and practice of the teacher is just as crucial to the development of the disciple as is the specific information that is imparted. Jesus didn't just *talk* about compassion for the poor, he acted it out. He loved his enemies. He gave a living example for his disciples to follow. This model is much more powerful than the mere intellectualism of the Greeks.

Greek View of the Body

Historically, the Greek separation of the human being into a good soul and evil body is called *dualism*. It is not a biblical model of humanity. It paints the human body as evil or even as the source of all human sinfulness. The concept of dualism invaded Christianity in the early years of the church as the Gentile world was converted. The people of the Roman Empire were steeped in

---

[43] Luke 10: 3–9

Greek philosophies. And because of their dualistic understanding of the human nature, ideas foreign to the Scriptures crept into the church. For example, *asceticism* is a world-denying philosophy, which equated denial of human pleasure and bodily appetites with the rule of reason over the "lower nature." This achievement of intellectual control over the body made those who practiced it seem superior to other men. From the ascetic philosophies of the day, we can see how the Gentiles would regard monks as "holy men," or as holier than other people. When ascetic philosophy invaded the church, we can also see how a dual class of Christian citizenship evolved: if truly holy people denied the body through celibacy and continual fasting, then those who were married and who ate food on a regular basis must be lesser Christians. Within this dualistic thinking is an unspoken suspicion that the body is somehow evil and should be despised. Such fears infected the church and are still with us today. But the Scriptures do not say holiness comes through celibacy or through fasting. Holiness comes through faith in Jesus Christ!

For a Christian who has inherited this Greek dualistic picture of Man, even his good desires for physical affection and sexual intimacy in marriage seem somehow wrong and evil. But in the Creation, God created the human body and called it part of a "good" creation! He gave Adam a wife as a sexual and emotional partner because it was not good that Adam be alone.[44] Even before the Fall, God said the two would become one flesh, and commanded them to "be fruitful and multiply."[45] The sexual union of Adam and Eve was part of his plan from the beginning. How then could the body and its desire for union be evil? It is not. It was created good, and holiness has nothing to do with hatred of the physical body.

The Bible's Use of "the Flesh"

We also get confused about the nature of the body because of the bible's use of the word "flesh" to describe sin. We logically think that the word "flesh" means the physical body, but it does not. It means something else entirely. The "fleshly nature" described in

---

[44] Genesis 1 & 2
[45] Genesis 1:28; 2:24

the bible is the desire to be independent from God. This desire to be independent can be manifested in our physical bodies through sexual immorality, but it can just as easily be manifested through pride, arrogance, stubbornness, or a critical and judgmental attitude. All of these attitudes are also called "works of the flesh." The best modern translation of "sinful flesh" would be "stubborn self-will." The physical "flesh" of our bodies is good, or at least it was created that way; but through the stubborn rebellion of our "flesh," we can use our bodies in an unholy manner.

In contrast to the dualistic thinking of the Greeks, the Hebrews understood a human being to be created with three separate parts linked in an inseparable unity: the spirit, the soul, and the body. All of these parts of a human being were good because God created us that way.

A Diagram of Human Nature

In order to understand the operation of faith in our lives it is necessary that we see human nature from a biblical perspective. Faith does not operate in the soul of a man, *as the Greeks would have believed*. Faith is a function of a man's *spirit*. Faith is the response of our *spirit* to the Spirit of God as the Holy Spirit influences us. We are vitally linked to God *through our spirit,* not through our soul. Our soul, our personality, is affected by this union, but it is our spirit that is given new life by the Holy Spirit through rebirth. For this reason, God is called the "Father of spirits," (Hebrews 12:9). Our spirit is reborn, and over time, our soul is conformed to the image of God as we grow in Christ.

Because this explanation of human nature is rather complex, I will put it in outline form: Spirit, Soul, & Body. (Please refer back to the diagram on page 53.)

1. The Spirit

The first of the three parts of a human being is his *spirit*.[46] In Genesis,

---

[46] Because the Hebrews did not have the full revelation of the nature of the Holy Spirit, they identified the physical characteristic of breathing with a spiritual reality. The Spirit of God was called "the breath of God," and in Hebrew, the word for breath, "ruach," is the same word as the word "wind" or "spirit."

God breathed into "the man" the Spirit, and "the man" became a living being. The Spirit of God was imparted to Adam through the breath (spirit) of God. As long as Adam was in relationship with God, the Holy Spirit was *in* him, and Adam had life.[47] But, when sin came, this relationship to God through the Holy Spirit was cut off, and Adam became spiritually separated from God. His human spirit was cut off from the source of life, and it lost the divine power of God. He became spiritually dead. God continued to sustain Adam's physical life by the abiding presence of the Spirit *with* man, but the Spirit of God no longer resided in Man.[48] Finally, when God withdrew the sustaining presence of the Holy Spirit from the man, the man dies physically.[49]

In the three-part nature of the human being, *the spirit has a particular function* just as the mind does. Cut off from life of God, the spirit does not function like it should, but a remnant of its former nature can still be identified. You can identify the operation of the human spirit by certain words we speak. Just as words like "I feel" identify our emotions, words like "I believe" or "I don't believe," reveal the characteristics and operation of a person's spirit. *Belief* is a function of the human spirit, just as logic and reason are functions of the human mind.

Because the function of the human spirit is so poorly understood, we often confuse human reason with faith. We think that understanding God's Word is the same thing as believing it, but the two are not alike. For example, I may *know* that Jesus said I can ask for "anything" in prayer, and receive it, but I may not *believe* that God will give it to me. This example highlights the difference between reasoning and believing. Jesus did not say I would receive answers to my prayers simply by understanding God's Word or by agreeing that the Word is true, I must also believe it in my spirit:

> *Therefore, I tell you, whatever you ask for in prayer, believe that you have received it, and it will be yours.*
> —Mark 11:24, NIV

Just like the brain is the organ of thinking, *the spirit is the organ of belief.* However, it is far more difficult to operate with belief than

---

[47] Genesis 2
[48] Genesis 6:3
[49] Psalms 146:4, Luke 23:46, Job 34: 14–15, Ecclesiastes 12:7

it is to use our human reason. An unsaved person can still think and reason, even though he does not believe in God. Only someone who is reborn through the Spirit of God has the capacity of belief restored fully to his human spirit. For this reason, there is a great difference between those who are in Christ and those who are not. The unsaved person will only be able to rely upon reason and emotions, or powers of the human soul, while a person who has been born again by the Spirit of God will be able to rely upon the Holy Spirit who communes with his human spirit.

2. The Soul

The spirit is an essential part of the human being, but it is not the whole human nature. The second part of a human being is his *soul*, which includes the characteristics that make up our personality. The soul of "man" is made up of three parts: *the mind, the will, and the emotions:*

a) The *mind* is that area we normally consider to be a person's reasoning ability, his thought life, and his imagination.[50] One of the easiest ways to identify that part of our personality is by our words. When a person says, *"I think ... "* usually he or she is speaking from his mind. With the mind, we may understand the Scriptures or figure out a problem in mathematics, but the mind is not the source of our faith, it is meant to be a servant of it.

b) The *will* is the second part of our personality. It is where we make decisions and choices. It is usually identified when we say things like, *"I will, I won't, I don't want to, etc."* From a biblical standpoint, the will has much more to do with our sinfulness than our body does. With the will, we refuse to obey God or we choose to obey him, and with the will, we choose to believe God's Word or reject it.

---

[50] Because the Hebrews did not know what part of the body was the seat of reason, they identified thoughts as coming from the man's heart. But whether you identify the thoughts of a man coming from his heart or his brain; it does not make a difference in the overall picture of the human condition.

Jesus was the only one who ever obeyed the Father perfectly. He did not follow his own will, wants, or desires, but he went to the cross saying, "Not my will, but your will be done, Father." So too, with our will we must learn to submit to the will of God, for that is the battleground of our sanctification.

c) Our *emotions* are the third part of our personality. They are easily identified by phrases like, *"I feel ..."* Our emotions can fluctuate like a roller coaster or can be steadfast, depending upon our personality. Emotions that are common to us usually define our personality: we can be known as happy and joyous, solemn and serious, depressed and despairing, or simply psychotic, which means we don't know what we are feeling.[51]

3. The Body

Finally, the third part of the human being is the *body*, often called *the flesh*. The body has appetites, like the Greeks suggested. Hunger, thirst, sexual desire, and the desire for warmth are all aspects of the human body. None of these desires are bad in themselves.

There is no area of greater confusion than in the phrase the "desires of the flesh," especially because the way Paul used it seems to imply that our physical desires, especially our desire for sexual intimacy, is a desire of the flesh. But that is not at all what Paul was saying. Did you know that the word in Hebrew for desire and lust is the same word? It is not desire that is bad, but the object of the desire can be. To want a wife or a husband is not a bad thing, but to want someone else's spouse is! The natural and good desire for a mate is a God-given thing. God created us originally to be one with another human being, so the desire itself cannot be a bad thing, no matter how powerfully we want that fulfillment, but to desire to mate with everyone and everything is lust!

Lust is the perversion of a good desire. It is taking a natural

---

[51] For most of my life, I was run by my emotions. Even when I knew better, my emotions were more powerful than my intellect. To have that inner conflict of emotions vs. reason is hard, and you can understand why the Greeks thought that if only you could rule your emotions through reason, you could be a whole person. But the power of the intellect alone is not as strong sometimes as our emotions.

desire that God gave us in creation and trying to satisfy that desire through physical means alone, rather than by the Spirit. The lusts of the flesh are the fruits of an untamed life. The soul that is not governed by the Spirit of God will be consumed with desires. Those uncontrollable or perverted desires, whether they are in the body, the will, the mind, or the emotions, are the "desires of the flesh," which Paul said are against the Spirit of God.

✣

So to summarize: we were created in the image of God. Included in this image are the spirit, which is the life of a human being; the soul, which is the three-part personality; and the physical body. God created us with all these parts and called it "good," but when sin entered the creation, *sin corrupted every aspect of the human personality.* Desires for food, sexual union, and comfort became uncontrollable or corrupted to lust. The mind, which was made to learn from God, became corrupted to such a degree that it could not distinguish between the truth of God and the lies of Satan. Our reasoning became illogical. Our knowledge became corrupted through arrogance, fear, and pride. Although the mind was not totally destroyed, it became seriously impaired. Our will, which had been obedient, became rebellious, stubborn, and selfish. Finally, our spirit, which had been living in union with the God of Life, was cut off from the life-giving presence of God. Our spirit became dead on the day of Adam's transgression. Before the Fall, Adam would respond to God with belief; after the Fall, his spirit would respond with unbelief.

Faith Under Separation

It is very hard for a person cut off from a living relationship with God to believe God. A person cut off from the Holy Spirit will fear God's judgment, so the natural human tendency will be to *run from God* rather than seek him. Feelings of guilt, anxiety, and condemnation will rule over a person's spirit through fear. Faith will not be the natural response to God in the unsaved person. Because of fear, faith will be unnatural! Doubt and unbelief are as natural to the unsaved person as death and disease are natural to the body in a fallen world. Therefore, there is a powerful struggle going on in a reborn Christian as he or she wages war against fallen human nature, which is why the bible says that by faith we *labor* to enter the rest of God. We are in a battle to cast off the old fears and unbelief which ruled our human nature before we came into fellowship with God. We are conforming our souls to the new relationship we have with Jesus Christ by the Spirit who now lives within us.

Sins and the State of Sin

It is also important to note that although sin is visible in concrete acts like murder, rape, and robbery, sin is also the state of being cut off from a living relationship with God. Therefore, "sins" are the individual deeds we do, but *"Sin" is the state of being cut off from God.* When a person is born again, his dead spirit is made alive and restored to the original relationship that Adam had with God before the Fall. To be reborn or "born again," according to the bible, is to receive the Holy Spirit into our being. It is being made "alive together with Christ." Therefore, when we are born again, we are "saints" because a Holy God is now living within us. We are no longer in a state of Sin, but we can still commit individual acts of "sin" through disobedience and unbelief.

However, a "sinner," according to the New Testament, is someone who does not have the Holy Spirit. Such a person cannot help but "sin" because there is no life in him. His spirit is dead, and pride, envy, fear, and the like are natural characteristics of a dead spirit. Actual "sins" are always going to be committed by someone who is not in Christ. Why? Because if a person is not in Christ, his spirit is dead and unbelief will arise out of that broken relationship with God. The deeds motivated by unbelief will naturally be sinful and unacceptable to God. Since unbelief is sin, those actions which arise out of unbelief will likewise be sinful.

For example, selfishness arises out of the fear that you will not have enough for yourself. Selfishness may express itself in greed and dishonesty, whereas freedom from self-concern produces generosity. The root will produce the fruit. If fear is the root, the fruit cannot be pleasing to God.

Let me show you another diagram:

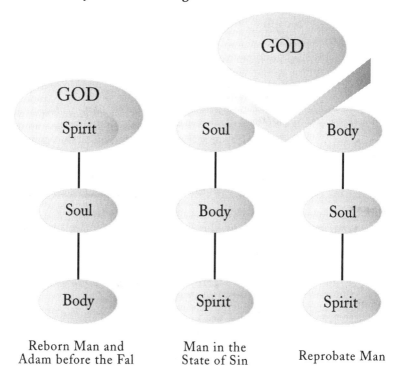

Three Types of Humanity in Relationship to God

In the picture we can see the unity of God with humanity before the Fall in Eden. Adam's spirit and God's Holy Spirit were in union. Since Jesus came to restore the creation to original unbroken fellowship with God, this diagram is also a picture of saved humanity after the resurrection of Jesus from the dead. After his resurrection, Jesus "breathed" upon the believers and said,

"Receive the Holy Spirit."[52] Just as God "breathed" life into Adam, so Jesus now "breathes" the Holy Spirit into us who believe. We are reunited with God by the "divine nature"[53] of the Holy Spirit, who is living inside us and in union with our human spirit.

Uncontrolled Sin – a Life Out of Order

For those who are not in Christ, we see two possible lifestyles: the *State of Sin* and an even more degenerate state called *Reprobation*, which will be described later.

The normal *State of Sin* is to be ruled by one's own personality: one's own will, one's own feelings and emotions, and one's mind. This is the common state of rebellion in which most of humanity finds itself. It is to be ruled by Self or Ego. A common attitude which reveals this rebellion is visible in such expressions as: "I am in control of my own life and I will do things my way. No one is going to tell me what to do!" True to the temptation of Satan, people with this mindset have made themselves god in some way. They worship at the altar of self-will. The problem these people have is that they are often in conflict with themselves and cannot do a thing about it. They may want to be ruled by their intellect, but are ruled by their emotions instead. They may want to be happy, but may live with constant depression. Their Ego is out of control and they cannot govern themselves. For example, a woman may want to love her neighbor, but she cannot get over a resentment and anger she feels over something the neighbor said ten years ago! She may want to forgive, but she cannot. In all her conflicting wants and desires, her will is blown about by her changing emotions and thoughts. Like so many who are burdened by their emotions, she tries to do a good thing but does an evil thing instead: "The good that I would do, I do not; and that which I do not want to do-I do!"[54]

The natural "man" in the State of Sin does not have the Spirit of God to give life and strength to his human spirit. Rather than being ruled by the good desires, this man is at war with his own passions. He cannot bring order to his emotions nor can he control his thought life. The irony of sin is that we want to be our own god,

---
[52] John 20:22
[53] 2 Peter 1:4
[54] Romans 7:19

but in the end, we cannot even govern ourselves! The personality, corrupted by sin, is hopelessly in disorder, and only the Spirit of God can restore a human being to the healthy state that God intended for us in Creation.

The Greeks were wrong about the strength of the mind. It is not just ignorance and passions at the root of human sinfulness; if that were true, just knowing the truth in your intellect would make you good. But the mind itself is corrupted by the power of sin. The biblical model paints a picture of man's will in rebellion *because* his spirit is cut off from a relationship with God. The rebellion pollutes the mind and makes it weak. In the State of Sin, a man cannot heal himself. He cannot completely control his own actions. He may *know* that he should love others, but he cannot. He may *feel* hate in his heart towards others instead, and he is helpless before his own emotions and cannot *do* what is right.

The Remedy for Life Long Bondage

The book of Hebrews says that humanity, before Jesus, was subject to a "life long bondage" of sinful rebellion because of fear of death, judgment, and rejection.[55] If you know how much it hurts to be rejected by someone you love, just think how unsettling it is for your spirit to be uncertain of whether God, your Creator, loves you. The fear and anxiety of uncertainty causes all sorts of rebellious behaviors in us.

Therefore, the fulfilment of our need is not just right thinking, but a renewed relationship of love with God. God already loves us. That is not the problem. The problem is that we do not naturally love God. We come into a loving relationship with God only by being "born from above"[56] by the Holy Spirit. This rebirth of our spirit communicates to us the ability to love God. By taking away our fear, we can then approach God in faith with love.

God made us in such a way that can only find this new relationship of love with him through Jesus Christ. Jesus said, "No

---

[55] Hebrews 2:15

[56] John 3:7– The words "born again" can also be translated as being "born anew," or "born from above." When Jesus said, "you must be born again," he was speaking of a spiritual reality of being born of the Holy Spirit of God. Nicodemus did not understand what Jesus was saying, and so he interpreted it in an earthly way of being born physically again.

man comes to the Father except by me."[57] So, for us to become one with God, we need Jesus Christ. It is only by and through Jesus that we receive the Holy Spirit, and the Holy Spirit frees us from fear of death, judgment, and rejection. *Since Jesus is gentle and will not force himself upon you, if you want the Holy Spirit, then ask Jesus to forgive you for trying to run your own life. Ask Jesus to be your Lord; then the Holy Spirit will be given to you. A rebirth of intimacy with God will be possible to you through the Holy Spirit. Healing can then come to your whole person, and order can begin to flow to your troubled personality.*

Jesus is the friend who brings us the presence of God. He is the answer for our needs, and faith is the means by which we receive him. There is no other way. Jesus is the only way we can escape the state of being cut off from God.

From Sin to Reprobation

Those who refuse to seek the presence of God eventually degenerate into an even worse state. The second state of fallen humanity is sometimes called *reprobation,* or being *reprobate,* which means that the personality of a man is in such disorder and so degenerate that rather than being ruled by his self-will, his emotions, or his mind, he is ruled by the lusts and impulses of his body. This disorder is so great that it is sometimes called "lawlessness." If you look around our society today, the evidence of the total depravity of humanity is clearly visible. It is now common to hear of murders taking place for no reason – except the murderer wanted to know the pleasure and the thrill of killing another human being. Such crimes are evidence of a reprobate culture. What it shows is a society without conscience. A person without conscience does not know right from wrong, or if he does know the difference, he does not care. As a culture declines, increasing numbers of the society fall into a reprobate condition.

Other examples of a reprobate society are the killing of children

---

[57] John 14:6

and the unborn, an increase in homosexuality,[58] and hatred of the church for its moral teachings and for its witness to Jesus Christ. Rather than being free, the people who fall into this state are in bondage to their own passions and cannot by any means escape, except by the power of Jesus Christ, if they will turn to him. They are ruled and governed by their impulses and compulsions. They claim to be free and revel in their depravity, but they are slaves to their own bodies and cannot break free from their behaviors.[59] When the reprobate rule a society, that society cannot survive for very long.

Summary

To summarize again: we can see from the diagrams that a person who is not in Christ will be motivated by unbelief in every area of life because his spirit is cut off from God. Without Christ within, no real righteousness or sanctification is possible. In this state of sin, the human spirit is empty of God, and the soul acts out in deeds of rebellion, motivated by the fear of death. Union with God through Jesus Christ is necessary to change this condition of separation from God, for then the Holy Spirit will join with the human spirit to bring God's life to us.

☦

The Next Step – Renewing the Soul to God's Truth

Simply receiving the Holy Spirit does not, by itself, allow us to walk in our sanctification. Faith is still required. Faith is not a one-time event. It is a continuous lifestyle. Although a person's spirit is reborn when he receives Jesus Christ as his Lord, his soul, *his personality,* is not reborn! His soul still retains all the memories of past experiences of rejection, all the striving, all the insecurity, and all the thought patterns of doubt and unbelief it had before. Therefore, a one-time experience of being born again will not instantaneously undo all the damage that a lifetime of sin

---

[58] Romans 1: 18-32
[59] 2 Peter 2:19

and rejection has done. That is why the soul, especially the mind and the emotions, must be *"renewed"* over time.[60] This renewal is God's goal for us, and he is at work in us, reforming and remaking us into his image through the circumstances we face in life.

I said before that this process of renewing the mind and emotions is how we labor to enter "his rest." Our mind is the battlefield, and God is trying to teach us of his love. God desires to sanctify our minds in the truth, but the devil wants us to doubt God and turn away in despair, hopelessness, and unbelief so that we will live our lives in fear. Our mind is the battleground. It is a struggle of belief vs. unbelief. We either believe God's Word is true and that he has finished the work for us, or we do not believe his Word and fall back into doubt, fear, and the striving of our flesh.

Sanctification of our soul, then, includes having our mind renewed to the truth of what Jesus Christ has done for us. Our mind can be sanctified,[61] and if it is, we will rest in Jesus' work. The labor we face is letting our mind be conformed to this truth. Jesus said we would be sanctified by the truth of God's Word, and that, by knowing the truth, the truth would make us free.[62]

So we have a decision to make: whether we are going to believe God's Word and rest in Christ, or whether we will let our past experiences and our emotions be our "god" and rule over us. The truth is we have been sanctified by the work of Christ, regardless of how we "feel." If we don't "feel" sanctified, then it is our emotions that must change, because God's Word does not change. When we are sanctified in the truth, we will believe God's Word in spite of how we feel. If we decide we believe God, then the struggle we face is to bring our soul, with its thoughts and emotions, under the dominion of God's Word. Rather than be governed by what we think or by how we feel, our thoughts are to be governed by the Word. The soul is to be brought into order, underneath our spirit, as God intended. Our spirit is to be governed by the Holy Spirit, and our body is brought into subjection as well.

---

[60] And be not conformed to this world: but be ye transformed by the renewing of your mind, that ye may prove what is that good, and acceptable, and perfect, will of God. (Romans 12:2, KJV)

[61] Sanctify them in the truth; your word is truth. (John 17:17, NRSV)

[62] Then you will know the truth, and the truth will set you free." (John 8:32, NIV)

Sanctification then, is not doing good deeds, *but destroying thought patterns and strongholds within us that resist the knowledge of God.* Sanctification is taking captive the thoughts of the mind which are rebellious, proud, and an obstacle to intimacy with God. Sanctification is destroying the proud thought patterns which lead us to justify ourselves through good deeds. It is destroying our fleshly desire for a holiness that is not based in Christ's righteousness. It is destroying our desire for independence from God. It is destroying a desire to add some work to the cross. It is resting in God and surrendering our attempts to be good. Sanctification is looking away from ourselves and looking completely, utterly, and totally to Jesus for all that God requires of us. It is knowing the truth about who Jesus is.

In short, **sanctification is disciplining our mind against the lie of Satan when he tells us that we can become righteous through our good deeds. Sanctification is standing in the truth that Jesus Christ is our righteousness. It is he who sanctifies us and makes us holy.**

Chapter Six

A Personal Testimony: The Spirit's Power

There is therefore now no condemnation for those who are in Christ Jesus. For the law of the Spirit of life in Christ Jesus has set me free from the law of sin and death. For God has done what the law, weakened by the flesh, could not do: sending his own Son in the likeness of sinful flesh and for sin, he condemned sin in the flesh, in order that the just requirement of the law might be fulfilled in us, who walk not according to the flesh but according to the Spirit. For those who live according to the flesh set their minds on the things of the flesh, but those who live according to the Spirit set their minds on the things of the Spirit. To set the mind on the flesh is death, but to set the mind on the Spirit is life and peace.

–Romans 8:1-6, RSV

If I could give you any testimony that would encourage you, I hope it is mine. I was (and still am!) so deeply grieved by my own sin, by my actions and by my attitudes of heart, that I wanted to be perfect before God. I wished to escape all aspects of sin so that I would be pleasing to my heavenly Father. My problem was that when I looked to discover some holiness in myself that would merit perfect communion with God I always found more sin. I thought that if I could just uncover every sinful attitude and confess it, then I would be perfectly clean and could dwell in uninterrupted fellowship with God. But the more I looked inside myself, the more sin I was able to find. I found that rooting out sin inside one's own soul is like killing cockroaches: when you turn on the light in your kitchen, they are everywhere. You can stomp on them all and kill everyone, but if you come back five minutes later, there they are again: creeping out of every crevice and dark corner. You can never get them all.

Endless self-examination will not root out every occasion or occurrence of sin. It is a discouraging process. The more we focus on ourselves, and our problems, the more we take our eyes off of Jesus. The irony of all this self-cleansing is that you and I are so disfigured by the character of the sin within us that we don't even know what is really wrong with us. We may be trying to get rid of a bad temper, but the root of our anger may be from some rejection we have received; we may be trying to heal a symptom and not even aware of the real disease within us. I have often found that to be the case. But Jesus is the Master Surgeon who knows what is really amiss, and he has the skill to set it right.

When I finally recognized that there *will never* be any good in me, I came to the point where I could fully trust Jesus. Rather than live in some pretended perfection, I now live in a constant state of confession, acknowledging my sin before God. When I look for righteousness, I do not look within myself; I look to Jesus *alone*. The Scripture says we have been made the righteousness of God in Christ, and that is true. However, it does not say that we are good, only that Jesus, who is good, now lives in us. He is our righteousness. This revelation of his righteousness creates great freedom in me. When the Accuser comes and says, "You did this and this and this wrong," I say, "You are right. But Jesus paid for that sin. He is my righteousness."[63]

I have found that I am able to rest completely in Jesus when I stop trying to defend myself and stop trying to perfect myself before God. When I acknowledge that the only righteousness I will ever have is Jesus, I am able to rest in the presence of God. My continual confession of my lack of righteousness allows me to trust completely in Jesus and rest in his righteousness. My surrender of *my* attempts to perfect myself has brought me to the place of complete trust. I am no longer afraid of finding sin inside myself because, every time guilt arises, I immediately point to Jesus and away from myself. I am now at the same point of faith as when I first believed, completing the work as it began, "by hearing with faith."

---

[63] It is because of him that you are in Christ Jesus, who has become for us wisdom from God– that is, our righteousness, holiness and redemption. (1Corinthians 1:30, NIV)

If there is any such thing as maturity in Christ, it is a deepening trust in Christ and his righteousness as a substitute for our lack of it. Maturity does not mean being more righteous before God, it means trusting Christ's righteousness more completely. So, the very act of surrendering our attempts to attain perfection puts us in the position of being able to abide in the intimacy with Jesus that our souls so desire. Our testimony is this: "I have no righteousness except Jesus. There is nothing good in me, and there never will be. I look not to myself for any good, but only to Christ who dwells in me."

I would not be completely honest with you if I did not tell you about certain events that took place in my life which allowed my faith to become more secure. Soon after I was saved, the issue of Christian perfection came up because of my desire to be completely clean before God. I became aware of the incredible power of sin in my own soul as it affected my thoughts and deeds. I tried to attain the discipline of endless confession to cure myself, but I really had no understanding of how God could work to destroy the desire for sin in my life. I knew that I should not lust, but lust I did, and I was helpless to control my own actions. Confession heightened my awareness, but did nothing to stop the desire. I did not understand the power of sanctification by faith in Jesus.

I was brought to Jesus Christ through the ministry of the Baptists, and from what I was taught by them, I really had no hope for any practical experience of sanctification: "You confess your sins, you get saved, and remain in your lusts but confess it every day, and you hang on till Jesus comes." That may be an oversimplification of Baptist theology, but it is a fairly accurate summary of what I was being taught. The doctrine of salvation through rebirth was very well developed in the denomination, but there was no concept of the ongoing work of Christ who came to destroy the works of the devil in us. When John writes, "I write that you may not sin,"[64] and "Whoever abides in him does not sin,"[65] the Baptists I knew were at a loss to explain the meaning of those passages. I felt I was left to struggle against sin, but Christ was of no help to me. He was just

---

[64] 1 John 2:1
[65] 1 John 3:6

there to forgive me when I failed, but I was being left to accomplish righteousness through my own choices and decisions. I had no concept of how to rely on the Spirit's power.

This theological ignorance of God's power to bring transformation to our character dates back to the Reformation. Luther talked about faith as necessary to salvation, but he really did not have much to say about sanctification. He believed that you were saved by faith alone, but you remain a sinner until you die. You are to struggle against sin and trust Jesus to forgive you when you fail, but all this effort seemed to take place through the power of human strength, or the human soul. (That is a very loose summary of his views.) Luther was lacking a concept of how the power of God could be brought to bear on our lives in such a way as to deliver us not only from the power of sin but from the desire for it as well! Some said it was a work of Grace, by which they meant that they did not understand it.

I learned from Luther, but I found several Scriptures which imply that God has a plan to bring us to maturity in *this life* not just after death! We are to be "made perfect in love," and all fear is to be removed from our lives.[66] The just requirements of the law are to be "fulfilled in us, who walk not in the power of the flesh but in the power of the Spirit."[67] There is supposed to be some sign of the power of sanctification ending sin in our lives:

> *Do you not know that the unrighteous will not inherit the kingdom of God? Do not be deceived; neither the immoral, nor idolaters, nor adulterers, nor sexual perverts, nor thieves, nor the greedy, nor drunkards, nor revilers, nor robbers will inherit the kingdom of God. And such were some of you. But you were washed,* **you were sanctified,** *you were justified in the name of the Lord Jesus Christ and in the Spirit of our God*
> *- 1 Corinthians 6:9-11, RSV.*

There is no escaping the conclusion that God's goal for us *in this life* is some form of Christian maturity, which reveals Christ's character in us. Not only are we to be free from the power of sin, but the practice of it as well. Faith should have as its desire such

---
[66] 1 John 4: 17–18
[67] Romans 8:4

a goal; otherwise, our time between salvation and resurrection makes no sense.

The powerless theology I learned as a new believer in Christ left me with a problem: the reality of my sin and my inability to overcome it. Then, in an hour of desperation, when I had reached the end of my strength, I cried out to God for deliverance; I knew that I had no other hope than a miracle from Jesus. I was on the wrong side, with those who would not inherit the kingdom, even though I believed in Jesus! I could not do anything to change myself. It was at this point that people began to witness to me about the power of the Holy Spirit to do in us what we cannot do for ourselves. Some people call it being "baptized in the Spirit," some call it being "filled with the Spirit." I don't believe God cares what you call it or how you label it, only that you begin to rely completely on the Holy Spirit, as God at work in you.

Our ancient creeds and confessions state "We believe in the Holy Spirit, the Lord the Giver of Life, who together with the Father and Son is worshipped and glorified ..."[68] But in actual practice, I did not really understand the Holy Spirit nor did I give him the honor due to him. I have found that in many Christian circles, the Holy Spirit is treated as an afterthought, and no one really knows what to make of him. Even doctrines of the Holy Spirit are fuzzy and unclear. People do not know him as the personal presence of God, which he is. I found this experience of the personal presence and power of God, released in a "Baptism of the Spirit," was a turning point in my walk with Jesus. God became more real and more accessible to me, and the application of his strength to my situation became an easier thing...

---

[68] The Nicene Creed

Let me use another diagram to show you the difference between a saved person living in the strength of his flesh and one who lives by the power of the Spirit:

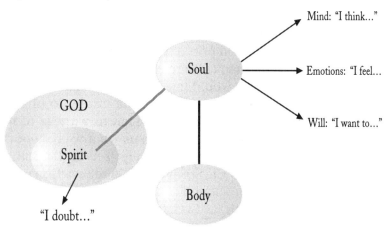

Saved But Carnal Christian - Relies on His Own Soul Rather than on God

This diagram is a picture of a man who is trying to live a godly life solely through the power of his own soul. He is relying upon himself and not upon God. He looks to his own intellect, will, and emotions, not to the Holy Spirit. He is cut off from the Holy Spirit's power as he tries to do things on his own. He gives orders to his body and emotions from his mind, but those orders are largely ignored. He does not understand the relationship to the Holy Spirit inside him, and he feels distant from God the Father. And although Jesus says to believe God and not to doubt, he has trouble with all sorts of doubts about God. He is the picture of the double-minded man who cannot receive anything from the Lord.[69] You could just as easily put the Pharisees in this diagram. They prayed seven times a day, they tithed, they did not commit adultery, but they were powerless to stop the hate filled attitudes of lust and judgment coming from their hearts! They were zealous for their outward

---

[69] James 1:6–8

righteousness, but they were ignorant of the righteousness that comes from God alone.[70] There must be something better for us, who are in Christ, than the shallow and wooden righteousness that comes from tightly controlled behavior! The power of the Spirit must somehow make up for the lack within us.

For me, I only began to trust Jesus for my righteousness when I was "baptized with the Holy Spirit." Please do not get hung up on labels. I received the Holy Spirit when I was born again, but then I struggled to complete Christ's righteousness in me through the strength of my flesh, and I failed. I did not know the reality of the Holy Spirit's power. To be baptized means to be immersed. When you are born again, you receive the Holy Spirit, but when you are baptized into the Holy Spirit, you are empowered with *his* strength.

When Jesus breathed on the disciples and said, "Receive the Holy Spirit,"[71] the disciples were born from above. Nevertheless, they were not filled with the power that was necessary to witness and evangelize. So, Jesus told them to "stay in the city (Jerusalem) until you are clothed with power from on high."[72] He knew that the disciples needed more than just their good intentions to carry out the tasks he had set before them. They needed the same mantle of power he received when the Holy Spirit came upon him after being baptized by John. If Jesus needed to be baptized with the Spirit to carry out his ministry on earth, then it is obvious we also need to be empowered by the Holy Spirit to do what God has called us to do. Not only do we need the anointing of the Holy Spirit to witness and evangelize, but we also need his strength to combat sin in our own lives.

Whether you call it being "baptized" or being "filled" with God's Holy Spirit, you and I both need him to be visible in our lives. If you find yourself at the end of your rope, looking more like a Pharisee than Jesus, then cry out to God for the empowerment of the Holy Spirit. Ask him to be all he wants to be in you so that you may be strengthened in your inner man, your spirit, through faith. For my testimony, I will tell you that the experience of the personal power

---

[70] Romans 10: 3
[71] John 20:22
[72] Luke 24:49

and presence of the Holy Spirit, which is ongoing, has enabled me to *believe* God more fully and trust him more completely. It was not enough for me to have a mental knowledge of Christ's righteousness, I needed to have a living and intimate relationship with his goodness, so that my faith might rest in him.

The Spirit Above the Emotions

Let me draw you another diagram:

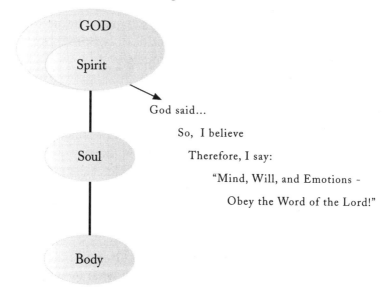

A Picture of Order: The Christian who obeys God by believing the Word of God. His Soul and his body align themselves under the dominion of his spirit which is directed by the Spirit of God.

From this diagram, we see a model of the Spirit-filled Man who is able to bring the mind, the emotions, the will, and the body into subjection to the Word of God.

The discipline of applying the Word of God to my circumstances, as I was enabled by the power of the Holy Spirit, did more to set me free from the prison of my own emotions than anything else I have ever done. Being an introspective person, prone to blaming myself for my problems, I really had to battle the depression I would often experience in my emotions. But there came a point when I had to decide whether I would be run by the instability of my emotions or whether I would bring the Word of God to bear on my emotions and command them to get in line.

We live in such a touchy-feely age, where everyone is so concerned about how they "feel," that we are in danger of being ruled by our emotions rather than objective reality. We all have had false perceptions which caused us to feel foolish emotions. We may have wrongly believed someone was mad at us or did not like us. We felt tension every time we were around this person, only later we discovered the person was not mad at us at all. He was tired or mad at something else or just so lost in thought that he ignored us. Yet, our false perceptions were ruling our behaviors and reactions.

In our relationship with God, those same false emotions can create a sense of division between us. We may not "feel" like God loves us, but Jesus said, "I will never leave you or forsake you."[73] So, he cannot have left us, no matter how we may "feel." Even when we don't feel God's love, the Scriptures say we are already "accepted in the beloved."[74] So, whom are you going to believe: your own changing and fickle emotions or God? Which will you allow to rule over you? Are your feelings going to be more truth to you than the Scriptures? Sometimes, you just cannot listen to your feelings; you have to ignore them.

What is important here is that the Holy Spirit inside us, through baptism into his power, releases in us the strength of the Spirit in our inner man so that we can bring those emotions into subjection to the Word. We renew our mind, our soul, to the truth of God's Word, and we choose to be governed by the Word instead of our feelings:

---

[73] Hebrews 13:5
[74] Ephesians 1:6

For this reason I bow my knees before the Father, from whom every family in heaven and on earth is named, that according to the riches of his glory he may grant you to be strengthened with might through his Spirit in the inner man, and that Christ may dwell in your hearts through faith; that you, being rooted and grounded in love, may have power to comprehend with all the saints what is the breadth and length and height and depth, and to know the love of Christ which surpasses knowledge, that you may be filled with all the fullness of God. Now to him who by the power at work within us is able to do far more abundantly than all that we ask or think.
– Ephesians 3:14-20, RSV

How foolish it is for us to be governed by the weakness of human emotions and to let our fears and hurt feelings be more of a determining influence in our lives than God's Word to us. In this culture, most people operate out of their emotions, but as believers, we should not conform to the character of this world.

The Pain of our Past

The difficulty many of us have in understanding and applying this discipline to our lives is that while our spirit is reborn into the image of God instantaneously at salvation, our personality (our soul) is renewed over time! It takes time to undo the years of damage that rejection and unbelief have done to us. It takes time to be healed of past experiences which cause painful memories. Our personality is real and it is not changed in a single day. We have all had experiences where we felt unloved and insecure. Our memories and experiences, both good and bad, have affected our soul. Since the soul is not instantaneously transformed through rebirth, we must be gradually healed through the patient application of the Word to our situation and by the healing balm of God's presence.

A clear example which demonstrates the healing character of Christ at work in our lives is in ministry to the saved homosexual.

Many times the experiences of rejection by a father or mother, the experience of abuse by an adult, or just the lack of affirmation, have left deep scars in the formation of the human personality. Just because someone gets saved doesn't mean that all those painful memories are instantaneously healed and that all the misdirected desires for love and acceptance are suddenly redirected in God's intended pattern. It takes time and patience to walk along side someone who has undergone those experiences and walk them through to the other side.

To demand instantaneous healing of all memories and damaged emotions from homosexuals simply because they have been saved is no more realistic than expecting instantaneous delivery from drug tendencies, lustful impulses, or selfish desire in the heterosexual who is newly saved. Yes, by God's grace, he does sometimes deliver people miraculously from many circumstances, addictions, and afflictions. But more often than not, most of us are healed gradually, and God does this for a purpose. We need to know we are loved, even with our failures and sins, before we can confidently begin the long and painful walk towards wholeness in the rest of their lives. If we don't learn this lesson of God's immeasurable love, we will walk on eggshells before God, constantly living the lie of a man on parole, which is, "God will only accept me if I live perfectly."

God has much love for us who, while walking towards obedience, slip and stumble. We cannot live in condemnation. We need to know we are not, will not, and need not be perfect; that failure is okay, and that God loves us anyway. Yes, the standard still exists, but it is to be approached by faith and in faith, not in constant fear of punishment. This knowledge of God's love is not an excuse to sin as we please or a license to abandon ourselves to lust. Willful sin, sins done on purpose, are harder to escape than sins we do under the compulsion and impulses of our human nature. However, to escape compulsive sin, we need to know the truth of God's love for us when we fail. Otherwise, fear and condemnation will keep us in bondage to the power of compulsive sin. Confession and forgiveness help us get free from compulsive behaviors, which enslave us. Being able to look to God, knowing he loves us still, even after we have sinned, allows us to go to God, so that he can deliver us.[75]

If we apply the Word of God to this situation, then the truth of the Word is that the person has already been sanctified from homosexual behaviors, affections, and tendencies. He has already been healed of damaged emotions. The process of sanctification is applying this truth to present circumstances, emotions, and even to the thought patterns that brought death and uncleanness. As the spirit man, or the inner man, comes to believe what God has already accomplished for him on the Cross, his mind and emotions will be renewed and be brought into conformity with the healing love of God. His desires will be redeemed and reformed to be like God's.

Part of this healing package is the hard work of forgiveness. It is necessary for the person who has suffered abuse to forgive the one who caused the abuse. As painful as that is, we are commanded to forgive, and forgiveness is necessary *for us* to be delivered from the bondage of sin and from old patterns of behavior. By acting in obedience to Jesus' command to "forgive," regardless of how we "feel" about the matter, God will open the doors for the healing of our emotions as well.

Forgiving Others

You may not have homosexual tendencies and perhaps you have not suffered any sexual or emotional abuse, but perhaps, in this discussion of forgiveness, the Lord has reminded you of people who have offended you or wounded you in some way. Perhaps you have wanted to forgive them, known that you should forgive them, but you just cannot bring yourself to do it, or you don't know how. Perhaps you are still angry with them, and you do not even want to forgive them. However, the Lord is dealing with you and you know you need to forgive. I'm going to teach you a truth that has set many people free from the wounds of the past. This truth is

---

[75] Do you not know that God's kindness is meant to lead you into repentance? (Romans 2:4)

the role of the will in the process of forgiveness.

First, you need to know a few things about healing and forgiveness. **Forgiveness is for *your* benefit**, not necessarily for the benefit of others. Forgiveness heals you. If you do not forgive others for how they have mistreated you, you will continually relive the wounds. You will live in the past, constantly being reminded of past injustices. You will relive them in your mind. Your emotions will fester and your thoughts will center on what happened to you, and you will rehearse and rehash it in your mind. You will not be able to get on with your life. You will react irrationally at times, not understanding why you get angry or upset over small things that happen.

Forgiveness heals you. It removes the pain of the past and lets you go on with your life. So, forgiveness is primarily for your health, peace of mind, and for your benefit. It is necessary *for you!*

Second, forgiveness is not saying that the person who wounded you was right. It is declaring that what was done to you *was wrong!* If a person has not wronged you, then they do not need to be forgiven. Only by identifying what was done to you as a sin, can you really forgive the other person. So, forgiveness is not saying, "It's okay that you hurt me. I deserved it." Forgiveness is saying, "What you did to me was *wrong!* And I didn't deserve it. You were wrong for doing that to me, but I forgive you."

Many people who have been abused find that the only way they can be healed is to stop taking the blame for what happened to them. It is common for those who have suffered abuse in childhood or rape to take the blame for the sexual, physical, and emotional abuse. They unconsciously think, "It was somehow my fault. I did something wrong and deserved it." This lie must be exposed for healing and forgiveness to take place. In order to be healed, if you have been abused, you must face the sin that was committed against you and declare it as a sin against you! Stand on your feet and say, "What *you* did to me was *wrong!*" Once you have faced the sin and identified it, you are now in a position to forgive it and be healed.

Third, forgiveness is saying, "Though you did me great harm, and you sinned against me, I choose to forgive you anyway." Just as Jesus did nothing wrong, but suffered for our sins and forgave us, in forgiving others, we too are choosing to act like Jesus and forgive those who caused us misery – even though they do not deserve it! We do not forgive because others deserve to be forgiven. We forgive because God said to.[76] It is a matter of obedience, not desire or emotions.

Fourth, and *this is important,* forgiveness is an act of the will, not an act of the emotions. Forgiveness is something we decide to do out of obedience to what God tells us to do, not something we do because we feel like we want to forgive. In fact, we may not feel like forgiving and may even feel like we cannot forgive; but the truth is, forgiveness is merely an act of the will, a decision. It can be done even if our emotions don't seem to be cooperating. The way forgiveness works is this: you choose to forgive someone by an act of your will, then God comes along and heals your emotions over time so that you later can feel the forgiveness towards those who harmed you. As you forgive, God will also heal your past and your painful emotions. That is how the process works.

Why is forgiveness so necessary? It seems that God knows that an unforgiving heart is a wounded heart. If you will not forgive others, it leads to a form of mental torture, where you are continuously reminded of past offences. Jesus described those who refused to forgive others as being bound over to torment by their own will.[77] Forgiveness is God's prescription for release from pain, and if we refuse to forgive, we are sentenced to a prison of our own making. No pardon or parole here! It isn't that God has refused to pardon us, but the condition for our release is that we agree to forgive others. If you want to be free from the pain of the past, it is time to forgive those who have harmed you. It is your choice.

Forgiveness is so important to your well-being and to your walk with Christ, that I include this prayer in the book. Many of you will find instantaneous release and healing simply by putting this

---

[76] Mark 11:25
[77] Matthew 18:21-35, (esp. 34-35)

prayer into practice:

Heavenly Father, forgive me for refusing to forgive others in the past. Either I did not know how, or I was unwilling to forgive. Thank you for forgiving me. As an act of obedience, I now choose to forgive those who have harmed me. I recognize that what they did to me was wrong, but I choose to forgive them as you have forgiven me in Jesus. (Now as the Lord brings to your mind various people, forgive each one by inserting his or her name and the sins in the blank spaces.)

In Jesus' Name, I choose to forgive you _____ for _____ to me and causing me such pain. I also forgive this sin _____, which you committed. Father, I now release _____ to you and to your care. I have forgiven him/her and ask you also to forgive him/her also, and do not hold this sin against him/her. I ask you also now to heal me of the pain this sin caused me, and I thank you that you will. In Jesus' Name, I pray. Amen.

If you begin to put this prayer into practice, you will begin to see healing take place in your heart. Forgiveness is a major step in the process of living in your sanctification in Christ Jesus.

✢

Summary

Obviously, this little book cannot be a complete guide to the application of the Word of God to the soul and personality of a believer. It is only a window to the task before us. The intent is to create an understanding of the operation of faith on the soul of humanity, so that actions, which demonstrate the fruit of the Spirit, can begin to flow through us who walk not in the strength of the flesh but in the power of the Spirit. Forgiveness is a way of removing one of the blocks in the soul, so that freedom of faith and the Spirit can flourish.

Let me say again, lest there be any confusion on the matter: we do not do good works to be good enough to gain God's favor and acceptance; good works flow out of us because we already have God's favor and acceptance. We don't do good works to get God to like us; we do good works because he already likes us!!! Our good works spring from thankfulness, praise, and the appreciation of what God has already done for us in Jesus Christ. There is no other foundation for works. And over time, as we come into fellowship with Jesus, our own soul, which is corrupted and damaged by this age, will show more clearly the character of Christ as we are transformed by his presence; and so, the fruit of the Spirit will become revealed in our lives. ❦

Chapter Seven

What is Faith?

The LORD said to Moses, "Send men to spy out the land of Canaan, which I give to the people of Israel; from each tribe of their fathers shall you send a man, every one a leader among them." –Numbers 13:1-2, RSV

Only, do not rebel against the LORD; and do not fear the people of the land, for they are bread for us; their protection is removed from them, and the LORD is with us; do not fear them." –Numbers 14:9, RSV

What is faith? Faith is knowing the will of God for you. Faith is not some innate power; it is a deep assurance of God's will, which produces rest within you. Faith is *not just* "knowing" the will of God in the intellectual sense, but a "knowing" with your entire being. It is knowing with your mind and trusting with your heart at the same time. Most "knowledge" comes merely from understanding what is written in the Bible, but there is a big difference between understanding God's general truth and believing that *this* Word of God applies to *you* today.

The Bible is not faith itself. The Bible is a road map to faith. For example, you can look at a map and see how to get from California to Washington D.C., but that does not mean that you've actually made the trip. You still have to travel the distance yourself. Faith does not come from the mind or from just knowing the words on the page. Faith comes from God out through your spirit. It has to be wrestled into existence and be made a reality to the whole personality. Just reading the Word gets you started on the path, but making it a reality is a life long process.

Faith, in the personal sense, depends upon knowing the will of God for your specific situation. For example, the general command of the Lord is to preach the gospel to all creation. But, out of a crowd of fifty people, God may want you to witness to a particular person because that person is ready to hear the gospel and is open to receive your witness. To know God's will for your life on a day-to-day basis requires intimate fellowship with Jesus. Faith, for the specific situations you face, does not come just by quoting particular verses of the Bible. A vital faith for everyday circumstances is developed through ongoing communion with the Father. In essence, faith is knowing what God has already said about the circumstances you face, and you gain that knowledge by hearing his voice.

Faith Equals Action

God told to the children of Israel to go up to the Promised Land and take it.[78] It was not his will for them to wander the desert for forty years. God led them straight from captivity in Egypt right to the borders of the Promised Land. He intended them to take the land immediately, but the people refused to believe what God had said. They refused to believe God's will for their lives. They wavered. Even after all the mighty miracles they had seen during the Exodus, they refused to believe that God could or would give them the Promised Land. They yielded to fear instead, believing God would not fulfill his promise. Even though they heard God say, "I give them the land of Canaan," they did not rely upon it. They did not trust God. They did not believe with their hearts, and because they did not trust God's word to them, they did not act upon it.

True faith and action always go together. You cannot have one without the other. For example, if you believe that a chair is strong enough to support your weight, you will sit in it; but if you don't think it is strong enough, you won't. If you believe the ice on a pond is thick enough to support you, you will walk on it; if you don't, you won't. Faith is like that. When you are convinced that God will do as he has said, then you will act in accordance with

---

[78] Numbers 13:1 & 14:9

what has been spoken. But that conviction comes from a different place than mere "head knowledge." It must be grounded more deeply than that. Faith comes out of an inner confidence that God will do as he said.

A Slave Mentality – Living in the Memory of Bondage

The children of Israel had something else at work in them, however, which was stronger than their trust in God's Word: a slave mentality. For years, they had been abused and tortured in Egypt. Because of this abuse, they had a hard time expecting good treatment from anyone. Even though God had delivered them marvelously, they were still unsure of God's desire to help them. *Their previous experience and past mistreatment was a more powerful influence in their lives than the Word of God.* Their previous experience was truth to them. Because they had been treated poorly, they expected the lash of a whip instead of the blessing of God. They had a very difficult time believing God really wanted to bless them. So, the Word of God became less important to them than their experience, and their past ruled over them.

This happens to many people today. Perhaps past sexual, physical, or mental abuse has created in you feelings of insecurity and inadequacy. Perhaps your father or mother was cold and uncaring or distant and belittling. Now, because you did not receive encouragement as a child from your earthly parents, you have a hard time believing God really wants to bless you. In some ways, your experience has become a powerful obstacle to you, and it is hard for you to believe in God's goodness. Or, maybe you were raised in an oppressive religious environment where the picture of God created in your mind is of a God who is more concerned about punishing sin than loving and redeeming sinners. Perhaps it is easier for you to expect punishment from God than loving encouragement. You are not alone. Many of us have been severely wounded by our past.

As we grow in faith, we learn to believe God rather than what our experience or emotions may tell us. Even our experiences have no right to exalt themselves over God. Yet, many people choose to be enslaved by their past and refuse to be released into the present. This decision to dwell on past experience leads to a double-mindedness that makes us unable to believe in God. When the Word says, "Beloved, I wish above all things that thou may **prosper** and be in health, even as your soul prospers," [79] we still have a hard time believing that God may want us to prosper and be healthy! But God is in the business of redeeming us from our past, and by his healing love, he will undo the pain and the lies of our experience, so that we may grow to believe and trust him.

Faith and Earthly Prosperity

Many people object to the idea that God wants us to prosper materially. They believe such ideas to be contrary to the ideals of the New Testament. But it is our Lord, Jesus, who said, "Give and it will be given back to you, more than you can handle."[80] It is true that we must be ready to surrender our earthly goods at a moment's notice, for his sake. We must value God above everything else, and we cannot worship money.[81] Our wealth cannot possess us, and we cannot live to satisfy our covetous greed, *but our lack of trust in God makes us greedy and selfish.* We become selfish because we do not trust God to provide for us. We fear to give money and food away because we do not believe God will take care of us! We do not believe we will have enough, and we subtly think God wants us either to starve or live in poverty. We are ready for a whip of punishment. We do not expect a blessing from his hand. Faith in God requires that we trust him to take care of us and provide for us; otherwise, we will become selfish and try to take care of our needs ourselves. For us to trust him for food and clothing, we need to know it is his will to provide us with these things. He will be faithful to provide us with our "daily bread."

The simplest summary of God's will for our life can be found

---

[79] 3 John 1:2

[80] Luke 6:38–see also 2 Cor. 9:6-8 for Paul's teaching on generosity.

[81] Matt. 6:24; James 4:4. But those who desire to be rich fall into temptation, into a snare, into many senseless and hurtful desires that plunge men into ruin and destruction. For the love of money is the root of all evils; it is through this craving that some have wandered away from the faith and pierced their hearts with many pangs. (1 Timothy 6:9–10, RSV) Little children, keep yourselves from idols. (1 John 5:21, RSV)

in the Lord's Prayer. Jesus told us to pray God's "will be done on earth as it is in heaven." Is there any sickness in heaven? Is there any disease? Is there any poverty? Is there any hunger? Is there any lack of love? Is there any unholy fear? Heaven is the place where God's will is done perfectly. Jesus wanted earth to resemble the perfection of heaven. So, God's will is for there to be no sickness, no fear, no disease, and no poverty here on earth. To pray according to God's will is to pray for health and prosperity, among other things. It is also to pray for all people to come to faith in Christ, for sure; but we are to pray for the necessities of life to be given us as well. Since we know it is God's will to provide for us, we can then trust him with our needs.

Faith and Health

Jesus is the perfect reflection of the Father.[82] He obeyed the Father's will perfectly. He revealed God's heart and desire for us. If Jesus healed everyone who came to him as part of his perfect obedience to the Father,[83] what do you think God's will is for us here and now? His perfect will is for all sickness to be abolished and removed from the earth, just as it is abolished in heaven! So, do we have a right to pray for sickness to be removed from our bodies with the confidence that it is the will of God? You bet we do!

Many people believe that God sends sickness and that, if you are sick, it is God's will. There are a few recorded cases in the Old and New Testaments where God "strikes" particular individuals who are in open rebellion and defiance of his will with sickness. King Uzziah was struck with leprosy for violating the sanctuary of God by offering incense, which he was not allowed to do. Miriam, Moses' sister, was also struck with leprosy for despising God's leadership through Moses. Pharaoh lost troops in the sea while trying to kill the Hebrews, and Korah was swallowed up by the earth for defying Moses' leadership. Bar-Jesus was struck

---

[82] He who has seen me, has seen the Father also. (John 14:9)
[83] Mark 1:32, Luke 4:40, Matthew 8:16

with blindness for opposing Paul's preaching of the gospel, and Ananias and Sapphira were killed for lying to the Holy Spirit. In all of these cases and in many more, it is open rebellion against God which caused such consequences. These are special cases of God's judgment upon those who despise his holiness. If that is the case with you, then repent. Miriam was healed after she asked for forgiveness. So you too will be healed if you also repent. God's will is for your healing, not for your destruction, and these special cases cannot be applied to common sickness and disease.

The sicknesses that most people suffer in this life *are not* God sent. They are the effects of a decaying creation or are attacks of the enemy on the believer. Most people fear that God has sent every illness to teach them a lesson. Our natural tendency towards guilt makes us feel like we have been rebelling against God and deserve whatever disease we get, but that is not what God thinks. That is not how God treats his children. Jesus considered sickness an oppression of God's people by the Devil, an oppression which Jesus came to destroy.[84] In fact, in the New Testament, the major suffering Christians experience is *at the hands of other people!* The suffering we are called to endure for Christ is not sickness and disease, but rejection and persecution and sometimes violence at the hands of those who resist God. God does not afflict his children with sickness and disease. Our call to suffering is external, not internal – at the hands of others, not as part of the course of nature. So, we have a right to expect healing from God, and every right to pray for it.

Some say that God wills everything that happens to us, so sickness is God's will for us. The Scripture says that God "works *in* all things for the good of those who love him,"[85] *but it does not say that all things that happen to us are good.* Even persecution is a mark of Satan's resistance to God's plan, not God's will. In persecution, hostility to God is being expressed through unbelievers as they resist the gospel. God's will is that they be saved, but he also gives them the freedom to resist the truth.[86] God wills their freedom, but not the evil they choose to do nor the harm they bring to others.

---

[84] ...how God anointed Jesus of Nazareth with the Holy Spirit and power, and how he went around doing good and healing all who were under the power of the devil, because God was with him. (Acts 10:38, NIV).
[85] Romans 8:28
[86] 2 Peter 3:9

He allows them to bring harm, but he does not desire it. So, in an indirect sense, because God wills their freedom, the persecution is within his will. But persecution is not good in itself nor does God will it as part of his plan for creation. God responds to the evil. The creative power of our God allows him to work good things out of evil events, but he has no part in bringing these evil things to pass. In the same way, sickness and disease are not the will of God for us, but are part of the fallen creation; and, thankfully, it is his will to heal us.

The Thorn in the Flesh – a Sickness?

Some have argued that Paul's famous "thorn in the flesh,"[87] is evidence that God does not heal every disease, but wills some sicknesses to keep us humble. This passage from Scripture makes a weak support for such a view. The thorn in the flesh is most likely not a physical mark, but Paul having to endure the indignity of being called a false apostle everywhere he went. Even in the churches Paul founded, "super-apostles" from Jerusalem challenged Paul's teachings because Paul did not require the Gentiles to follow Jewish customs. These people challenged Paul's right to be called an apostle because Paul had not traveled with Jesus on earth like the other apostles. They ripped apart and divided Paul's congregations everywhere they went and caused Paul endless heartache. They forced him to bear with "insults" and disrespect. Even more upsetting to Paul, these deceivers forced him to defend his ministry to the very people he led to Christ. He was hurt that the people, who should have known him the best, were so easily persuaded to doubt him and his ministry. However, what angered Paul the most was that these "servants of Satan"[88] turned the people's hearts away from a simple and pure trust in Christ to some other false gospel of works and laws.

No wonder Paul cried out to be delivered from this exasperating "thorn" which undermined his ministry to the Gentiles. However, God would not remove this "thorn" saying, "My grace is sufficient for

---

[87] 2 Corinthians 12: 1–10
[88] 2 Corinthians 11: 3–4,13–15

you to endure this. My power is made perfect in your weakness."[89] God saw the good that would eventually come from these attacks upon Paul's ministry. In fact, most of the New Testament was written in response to this "thorn." Paul used his letters to defend his understanding of God's grace in Jesus Christ. God's power was certainly made perfect in Paul's inability to overcome this handicap of opposition, and we are all the richer for his lack.

I know I am digressing, but this one passage of scripture about Paul's thorn is used to justify sickness and disease as God's will for all. However, an extensive word study of the way in which Paul uses the word "infirmity" in his letters seems to indicate that he is speaking not of sickness and disease, but of his humiliation and weakness in the face of others who taunt and ridicule him.

> *That is why, for Christ's sake, I delight in weaknesses, in insults, in hardships, in persecutions, in difficulties. For when I am weak, then I am strong.* –2 Corinthians 12:10, NIV

Even in the context of this passage, Paul compares his "thorn" of weakness to insults and persecutions, not to physical illnesses. Therefore, we will have a hard time defending sickness and disease as God's will from the New Testament, especially since Jesus only healed the sick and never gave anyone a disease.

I AM the Lord Who Heals You

In the Old Testament, God reveals his Name to the people of Israel when he uses the phrase "I AM." "I AM" is his covenant Name. It is his personal Name. To the Gentiles, he is "God," but to the Jews, he is I AM WHO I AM.[90] His Name is an expression of his sacred identity. In Exodus, when God says, "I AM the Lord *who heals you,*"[91] he is giving a promise to *be healing* to his people. As a sign of his covenant blessings, God promises to take away sickness and disease from their midst.[92] This covenant never ended, but was extended to all believers in the New Testament.[93] When Jesus stood and said, "Before Abraham was, I AM,"[94] he was identifying himself

---

[89] 2 Corinthians 12:9
[90] Exodus 3:14
[91] Exodus 15:26
[92] Deuteronomy 5: 33, 7:15, Psalm 103:3
[93] Galatians 3:14
[94] John 8:58

with the same covenant Name of God as in the Old Testament. That is why the Pharisees wanted to stone Jesus for blasphemy. He was calling himself the "I AM," which was God's revealed Name. Jesus was calling himself "God," and the Pharisees knew it. So, if Jesus is the same God as revealed in the Old Testament, then the covenant Name is still in effect. Jesus is the God who heals us.

The point is: if God identifies himself as *the God who heals,* how are we going to have faith in him if we do not know him as he is? If he says, "I AM Your Healer," and we reject it, how can we be said to have faith in God? We believe in a different god, a god who does not heal. To reject healing is to reject his Name, for he is the God who heals. He wants to be known as our Healer. If we expect sickness and disease from him instead, how can we come to him? Will we not rather run from him? How can you trust a God who wants to give you cancer? Sickness is not part of his Name or his Person. To believe otherwise is to believe in a falsehood about God.

Our God is asking us to believe him for who he is. He is asking us to accept him as he is: "For I know the plans I have for you," declares the LORD, "plans to prosper you and *not to harm you,* plans to give you hope and a future," (Jeremiah 29:11, NIV).

He wants us to know that he does not have the whip of sickness or the lash of disease to give to his people, but as his Name is healing, so is his desire for us. If we cannot trust him in these most simple and elemental things, do you really think we will be able to believe him for our sanctification?

The God Who Provides

Just as we have a right to expect healing from the hand of God, we also have a right to pray for food and clothing and shelter. For just as there is no illness in heaven, there is also no lack. We even have a right to pray for money beyond our own needs, for it is God's will that we be generous to the poor.[95] If we are poor, we cannot be generous because we cannot give what we do not have.

---

[95] 2 Corinthians 9: 6–15

Many people, who hate the message of "prosperity," are weighed down by guilt. They think they deserve the "whip" from God and not the blessing. They have retreated back into slavery. The problem with their view of money is that they believe it is more holy to be poor than to be able to help those who are poor. Rather than helping the person in the gutter get up and out of it, they would lie down with him and "feel" his pain. They would be "compassionate" and "caring," but totally worthless in accomplishing any long term good in the lives of those who need it. It takes money to help the poor. And if you cannot even feed yourself, how are you going to feed others?

The quickest cure for the guilt mentality that fears or hates prosperity is to give your tithe of ten percent to the Lord and give more money to help the poor; then, you will not feel guilty about having a little for yourself. God is a God of abundance, and his Spirit is the Spirit of generosity. He gives because he loves to give, and he wants us to be like him. God gives abundantly out of his abundance, not out of his lack. The generosity of those who have wealth is God's means of war on poverty:

> *But there will be no poor among you (for the LORD will bless you in the land which the LORD your God gives you for an inheritance to possess), if only you will obey the voice of the LORD your God, being careful to do all this commandment which I command you this day. For the LORD your God will bless you, as he promised you, and you shall lend to many nations, but you shall not borrow; and you shall rule over many nations, but they shall not rule over you. -Deut. 15: 4-6*

So why should we feel guilt if we are faithful to be generous with what we have? Why should we believe it is *not* God's will to prosper us when he said he wants to bless us?

Double-Mindedness

Nevertheless, though we know what the Word of God says about prosperity, we may not be fully persuaded *in our hearts* that it is true, that it is meant for us today, and that it applies to us in our circumstances. This confusion about applying the Word of God leads to a characteristic called "double-mindedness" in us. Double-mindedness resists faith. Double-mindedness is a characteristic which leads us into deception. We are deceived by it because we may *think* we believe God's Word in a certain area, but we may not really believe it at all. For example, we may *assent mentally* to God's Word where it says that he wants to bless us, prosper us, and to heal us of all our diseases, but still we may not fully *believe* it in our hearts. The error in our thinking is that we are more than just our intellect and our reason. We are spirit, emotions, and experience as well. Out of our spirit, through the heart, we believe, but our minds are the battleground.

Jesus said that if we ask anything in faith while believing it in our hearts, our heavenly Father would do it for us.[96] He said we could ask for anything from the Father and it would be given to us,[97] but we have trouble really believing those Words in our heart. It sounds too good to be true. Yet, we are to ask in faith without doubting:

> *But when he asks, he must believe and not doubt, because he who doubts is like a wave of the sea, blown and tossed by the wind. That man should not think he will receive anything from the Lord; he is a double-minded man, unstable in all he does. –James 1:6-8, NIV*

It is interesting to note that the word for double-minded in James is *di-psuchos*, which means "two-souled." The implication is that a person is in conflict with himself. He has two thoughts or two reasonings on an issue, neither one of them necessarily bad, but he just cannot make up his mind what he truly believes. For example, a child may not be able to decide whether to get a chocolate or vanilla ice cream cone. While he is waiting there to decide, probably driving his parents crazy, his indecision is a form of double-mindedness. He likes both, but until he chooses, he will not get either one. By the same token, a person may agree in principle that God wants his people to prosper so they can

---

[96] Mark 11:22–24
[97] John 16:23

be generous, but in his heart he feels that he is too sinful and unworthy to receive a blessing. That person will not be able to approach God in faith to ask for a financial blessing because he doubts that it is God's will for his life! He is double-minded. He doesn't really believe God wants *him* to prosper.

Faith requires not only that we be fully convinced in our minds of God's will for us, but that those areas of uncertainty in our hearts be rooted out and demolished. Only when those uncertainties are addressed are we able to break through a pattern of unbelief into true faith. Areas such as healing and financial provision may seem unrelated to such deep matters as sanctification and righteousness. But I find that it is impossible to really believe God on a consistent basis for the "spiritual" things if we are always worried about the necessities of life. Jesus said not to worry about clothing or food, because "your heavenly Father knows you need them."[98] He knew that if we could not trust our Father to be our provider, we would not be able to trust him with other areas of our life. Because we are physical beings as well as spiritual ones, we cannot divide the needs of our body completely from the needs of our soul. Jesus said, "Man does not live by bread *alone*,"[99] but he still knew we needed a certain amount of bread to survive, so he taught us to pray daily for bread. Faith for provision and protection are integrally related to faith for the deeper and more eternal things of God, and we need to learn to trust our Father in every area of life.

Poverty and Holiness

Sometimes our religious traditions make us unable to believe the Word of God. Because the medieval church was greatly influenced by Greek philosophy, it tended to identify the "passions of the flesh" with sexual and visceral appetites, rather than with a proud and independent will. The medieval remedy was asceticism. The monks established a pattern of "mortifying" the flesh through fasting, celibacy, and vows of poverty. The unwritten assumption communicated to the rest of the church was that these people were

---

[98] Matthew 6:25–34
[99] Matthew 4:4

"holier" than the average believer. The residue of that mentality is still with us. We are taught that Jesus was poor, and therefore, the unspoken message is that *if we want to be holy like Jesus, we must be poor also.* Now if we hold that message as one of our deep thoughts, when we pray for prosperity, somehow we will feel that we are praying against God's will, and therefore we will not have any faith in what we pray; for we secretly think, poverty is good and God wants us to be poor.

The problem with this religious thinking is a small fact: the Bible does not say that Jesus was a simple carpenter, but that he was a *"tekton,"* or a "builder." He was probably the equivalent of a building contractor.[100] The Gospel of Mark indicates Jesus probably had a home by the sea in Capernaum with a tile roof, unlike the more common flat-rolled mud roofs of the day.[101] And during his ministry, he had so much money flowing through his treasury that even though Judas was stealing from it, nobody missed the money. You can't have an entourage of ninety or more people going around with you and not have some money flowing through your hands. Just to feed that group would take quite a bit of cash per day to buy bread. And you don't need a treasurer if you only have ten dollars to your name. Jesus' ministry was well funded. Finally, although Jesus was born in a stable, he was not born there because his parents had no money for a room, but because there were no rooms left in the inn. The census had created a convention, and all the hotel rooms were booked. But we tend to think his parents were so poor they couldn't afford decent lodging.

In spite of all these facts of scripture, we still have trouble seeing Jesus as having more than enough to meet his needs. Yet don't you think he gave offerings, alms, and tithes? He never broke the Law. He was faithful under the Law and he was generous. Sometimes we need to reexamine our traditions so that we may open our hearts to believing God's Word. We don't need to be greedy, but we shouldn't be needy.

---

[100] George Wesley Buchanan, "Jesus and the Upper Class," *Novum Testamentum,* vol. vii, Fasc. 3, 1964, pp. 204–206.
[101] Mark 2: 1–15.

Faith is not Begging but is the Knowledge of His Will

Finally, faith is not begging or pleading. It is not trying to convince God to answer prayer. Faith is not approaching God with the reasonableness of your requests. I have heard it said that if you think by prayer you are going to get God to change his mind, you will never have faith, because God is unchanging. "Every good and perfect gift is from above, coming down from the Father of the heavenly lights, who does not change like shifting shadows," (James 1:17, NIV). Therefore, we cannot approach God, trying to change his mind. If God, the judge of the universe, does not want to do something, how in the world are we going to convince him to do otherwise? Faith, then, must come from another source.

We gain faith if we already know God's answer. The only way we can have faith is if we know his *already* spoken will and agree with what *he* has said. His will for creation has been written in the Book! It is our responsibility to know what he has spoken to us in his Word. Faith is not asserting our own will and trying to get God to agree with us. It is *understanding* what God's plan is and then saying *yes* to it with our hearts. Our knowledge of God's will for us, and for the creation, comes by the study of the written Word. Through knowledge of his Word, and intimate fellowship with the Father, we increase our faith and we put to death double-mindedness. As we come to agree with God, it is no longer *just* our wants and our wishes we bring before the Father; we come with the confidence of his will. We *now* know what *his* will is for us and for others. When we know that, we pray with authority, conviction, and power. We pray in faith because *we know* God is on our side and in favor of our prayers.

For example, you may want a million dollars and may pray to God for it, but unless God has spoken to you that it is *his* will for you to receive it, then you will not have the faith necessary to believe God without doubting. You may have a mental conviction of the rightness of your prayers, but that is not faith; it is mental effort. You might as well believe the moon is made of blue cheese. What you "believe" in your head does not change reality, and it certainly will not change God. Abraham had faith, not because he wanted a son, which he did, but because the Lord spoke to him first! *Abraham's faith was a response to what God had spoken to him.* God said he was going to make Abraham the Father of many nations, and Abraham believed God! Our faith is also a **response** to what God says to us. We just don't create faith out of thin air. We must hear, perceive, understand, and know what God wants to do for us. Our faith is a response to God. That kind of faith only comes through intimacy with Jesus.

In the Gospel of John, Jesus says that if we ask anything in his name, he will do it.[102] We can ask the Father for *anything!!!* When I was first in Christ, I tried to make that promise a reality. I asked for a lot of things that did not come to pass. I misunderstood the meaning of the Lord's Name. In the Bible, the phrase "in my Name" is not a formula we can chant to make God do something. We cannot get God to answer our prayers simply by ending our prayers with "for we ask in the name of Jesus." If God jumped every time we did, we could control God and get him to do our bidding. Faith is not a formula whereby we control God. Faith is a response to God. The phrase "in my Name," is shorthand for "in my presence." In ancient cultures, the Name stood for the whole person. It was the representation of the whole. In other words, a better translation would be: "If you are standing with me in the presence of the Father and you are abiding in my love and know my will, you can ask anything of me and my Father, and I will carry it out." This promise of God to answer all our prayers assumes a certain level of intimacy and fellowship with God. Jesus' promise depends upon a living, breathing relationship with the Father, so that it is easy for us to ask him for things and then expect him to carry them out.

I have found that when I am asking or praying for anything in faith, it is easy to believe. There is no strain or stress involved. But when I am not entirely sure of my prayer, when I am not fully convinced, and when I am walking only in mental assent or reasonings, then I am full of stress as I pray. There is no rest in

---

[102] John 14:13

me. I am anxious and I keep wondering when, or if, God is going to answer my prayers. In contrast, the Scripture says that there is "joy and peace in believing."[103] When faith is manifest, there is an ease about it. "Faith is the assurance of things hoped for, the confidence of things not yet seen," (Hebrews 11:1). When faith is manifest inside you, you don't have to "try" and believe. You just believe.

Hurt by Unanswered Prayers

More people are hurt and confused over this one issue than perhaps anything else in American Christianity. Many people, walking in the strength of their intellect alone, have confused mental assent with true faith and have acted in presumption. Not realizing that faith comes out of the person's spirit (the inner man), they have been badly hurt when they failed to receive answers to their prayers. Yet because of our western heritage, our culture confuses intellectual understanding of God's Word with true, developed, mature faith. I have made this mistake often. The easiest way to tell if you are operating in faith or presumption is to pray. If you are not confident and resting in the sure knowledge that Jesus has heard and answered your prayers, then you probably are not walking in faith. As you learn the difference between faith and presumption, God will lead you to a deeper trust in him. He will teach you of himself, so that you might come to faith.

‡

---

[103] Romans 15:13

Summary

You may disagree with me about many things. You may not be confident that God wants to bless you financially, physically, emotionally, and socially. You may believe that God wants you to suffer all sorts of disease and poverty. You are free to believe that. But I have found that it is hard to have faith in God for anything at all when I am not convinced that he has my best interests at heart. If giving me cancer is God's idea of an education, then I may have trouble seeking God! Why should I go to him, if all I will receive are the curses of disease, poverty, and starvation? I would rather run from him. Faith in God's goodness, and in his desire to care for and bless us, is essential to trusting God with all of our lives. If we fear rejection and condemnation, it will be hard for us to open ourselves before him to confess our sins.

Nevertheless, you may not agree with me about any of those things, but please agree with me that God wants you sanctified and holy!!! At least you cannot find anything in God's Word, no matter how interpreted, to disagree with that! Therefore, agree with me to believe that God wants you sanctified and holy.[104] He wants you to completely resemble his Son, Jesus.[105] He wants you to be free of sin and its character. At least have faith for that! And by faith, enter into the promises of God.

---

[104] May God himself, the God of peace, sanctify you through and through. May your whole spirit, soul and body be kept blameless at the coming of our Lord Jesus Christ. The one who calls you is faithful and he will do it. (1Thessalonians 5:23–24, NIV)

May the God of peace himself sanctify you entirely; and may your spirit and soul and body be kept sound and blameless at the coming of our Lord Jesus Christ. The one who calls you is faithful, and he will do this. (1Thessalonians 5:23–24, NRSV)

[105] Romans 8:29

Chapter Eight

WHAT IF I DON'T HAVE ENOUGH FAITH?

All things are possible to him who believes.
                                              -Mark 9:23

Condemnation and Sickness

Before I was a Christian, I never thought much about getting sick. If I got sick, I just endured it until I got well, and that was that. After I became a Christian and found out that God wanted me well, I started feeling guilty for *being* sick. Now not only was I sick, I felt guilty for being sick. It felt like the devil was saying, "You pathetic loser! If you only had faith, you wouldn't be sick!" I felt as if I were failing God because I didn't have enough faith to be made well, or so it seemed to me. If "all things are possible to the one who believes," my sicknesses proved that I didn't have much faith in God.

Perhaps you've heard that old lie yourself. Perhaps you've heard people say things like, "Mr. Jones wouldn't have died of cancer if he'd just had faith," or, "If you just had enough faith, you'd be well." I can't think of anything more unlike Christ than blaming the victim for being sick. First, the devil attacks the person with sickness, and then he tells the person it's his own fault! Talk about "kicking a man when he's down!"

Sickness and disease, we've discovered, are part of Satan's arsenal. They are part of his kingdom of suffering on the earth. One of the devil's strategies is to make us feel condemned and guilty so that we will not approach Jesus for relief. What better way to make us feel guilty than to make us sick and then make us feel like it is our fault for being ill! It is the devil's strategy to get the children of God to condemn themselves. The more we condemn ourselves; the more successful he is in his deceptions.

Even if the devil doesn't cause the sickness – even if it just part of the natural ills of this world – the devil still takes advantage of disease by heaping hot coals of condemnation on top of our heads. If he can make us feel guilty in the midst of our illness, so much the better! If he can make us feel like we deserve to be sick or like the sickness itself is our fault, he is pleased. Whatever works to destroy our faith and trust in God fits his strategy for success.

After I learned of God's desire to heal me and saw my failure to receive healing, I had to go to God and confess my weakness of faith. I said to him, "Lord, I know you want me well, but I can't seem to believe it. I don't have enough faith. I don't have the strength to make myself well." After I confessed my weakness, I found that all I could do was rest in the knowledge of this verse of scripture: "There is therefore now *no condemnation* for those who are in Christ Jesus."[106] Whether sick or well, we are not condemned, and we should not let the devil use sickness to divide us from the Father's presence and love. We should not succumb to a guilty conscience simply because we suffer as all people sometimes do. This world is a hostile place, and sickness is a thorn on the branches of this natural world. God wants us healthy and whole, that is true, but he isn't condemning us when we get beaten up by life.

After I faced down the condemnation, I did a little research into the Scriptures. The only people the Lord berated for their "unbelief" were the disciples, who should have known better.[107] Jesus never condemned the sick for being ill or judged them for not having enough faith. He recognized that those who were sick were in need of a physician. They could not help or heal themselves. They needed a healer. Jesus' response was one of mercy and compassion, and he healed them without judgment. We should learn from him how to behave towards the sick!

---

[106] Romans 8:1
[107] Matthew 14:31; 17:20

The Fallacy of the Mustard Seed

When Jesus corrected his disciples, it is interesting how he did it. After he taught them and trained them to heal the sick and cast out demons, he sent them out to do it.[108] It even says that he gave the disciples "power and authority over all demons and to cure diseases." So, when they failed to do what he told them to do, Jesus was a little frustrated with them. However, the words he uses to describe their failure do not mean what we often assume them to mean. In Greek, the word "unbelief" {*apistia*} literally means "no-faith." It wasn't their "little faith" that was the problem; it was their absence of all faith. They had no faith:

> *"Lord, have mercy on my son, for he is an epileptic and suffers severely; for he often falls into the fire and often into the water. So I brought him to your disciples, but they could not cure him." Then Jesus answered and said, "O faithless and perverse generation, how long shall I be with you? How long shall I bear with you? Bring him here to me." And Jesus rebuked the demon, and it came out of him; and the child was cured from that very hour. Then the disciples came to Jesus privately and said, "Why could we not cast it out?" So Jesus said to them, "Because of your unbelief; for assuredly, I say to you, if you have faith as a mustard seed, you will say to this mountain, 'Move from here to there,' and it will move; and nothing will be impossible for you."*
> *–Matthew 17:15-20, NKJV*

> *"And the apostles said to the Lord, "Increase our faith." So, the Lord said, "If you have faith as a mustard seed, you can say to this mulberry tree, 'Be pulled up by the roots, and be planted in the sea,' and it would obey you."*
> *–Luke 17:5,6, NKJV*

When the disciples asked for more faith, Jesus' response to them was not what they expected. He did not ask his Father to given the disciples more faith. Instead, he said to them, "You don't need more faith. If you have even the smallest amount of faith, it is more than enough to move mountains. Not a lot of faith, but any faith at

---

[108] Luke 9:2

all will do the work! Faith works. You don't have to make it work, or grow your faith, so you can accomplish things. You either have faith, or you don't. If you have it, you will move mountains and nothing will be impossible to you; but if faith is absent, nothing will be possible to you."

The mustard seed is the tiniest of seeds. It is hard to see and easy to overlook. In the First Century, the mustard seed's size was used to express something's smallness, like our word "atom." Jesus was comparing the invincible and dynamic power of limitless faith to the smallest thing possible. He was saying, in effect, if your faith is the size of the smallest atom, it is more than enough to get the job done. So, the problem isn't how much faith you have; it is what you believe. You have enough faith, but you are not believing God. You have faith in a lie. Your faith is working; it is just working in the wrong direction. Your faith needs to be redirected towards the truth and towards God, and then nothing will be impossible to you.

The Logical Box of Failure

There are a few Scriptures which make it seem as if the entire responsibility for faith rests upon our shoulders and our abilities:

> *If you believe, you will receive whatever you ask for in prayer.*
> *—Matthew 21:22*

> *Truly, truly, I say to you, he who believes in me will also do the works that I do; and greater works than these will he do, because I go to the Father.* *—John 14:12*

If you believe! The great "if" of Scripture that causes us to stumble! What "if" I don't believe? What then?

I used to think that if I could just believe enough, then I would do the mighty works of God. If I had *enough* faith, then I would be well; and not only I, but all whom I touched would be healed. Unfortunately, I wasn't healing others, or being healed myself; so, I realized that I must not have enough faith. If *only* I could believe!

There is a prison of the mind created by such thoughts about faith. The logic of this prison is a train of thought, which goes something like this:

> God asks me to believe in him and have faith. If I believe, then all things are possible, but if I do not believe, then God will not answer my prayers.
>
> But what if I lack faith? How can I ask for it, since to receive faith I have to believe I will receive it? But believing is my problem in the first place!
>
> No matter what I do, I cannot find my way out of this logical box, because I need something that I don't have in order to be healed and be made whole! God has not given it to me. He will not give it to me because I lack faith! He will only give it to me, if I have faith! It is hopeless!

If you have ever suffered from a long or incurable illness, or have known the pain of unanswered prayers, your mind may have run in circles around these promises of Scripture. As you can see, this reasoning throws us back upon ourselves to be our own saviors. Now, we save ourselves through our own faith. By faith, we can deliver ourselves from our afflictions and receive answers to all our prayers! What saves us is the amount of faith we have. If we don't have faith, we must learn it or earn it in order to be pleasing to God. And woe to us if we lack faith!

I used to believe that confessing verses of the Scripture and training my mind to rehearse Bible truths would bring me to the fountain of faith, where I could drink deeply and be satisfied. I believe these things no longer. After many years of striving to believe, I found that such labors of the mind do not produce faith. Fasting and prayer do not produce faith either, although those seemed like good, religious things to do at the time.

Many people teach that you must confess the Scriptures with your mouth until you believe in your heart. While there is benefit for training the mind to know the truth of the Scriptures – of God's desire to heal, to answer prayers, and to do miracles on our behalf

– much of this confession teaching is merely an exercise of the soul, or of the rational mind. It is a form of mental knowledge or mental assent to the truth. It is a form of soul power, not divine faith from our spiritual nature. Such prescriptions for verbal confession and Scripture recitation degenerate into a work of human performance: a mere work of the flesh. *Instead of relying upon God, we now rely on our own ability to believe God or upon our ability to recite Scriptures.* This is a perversion of true faith; for true faith brings a deep and utter dependence upon God.

Religious Mind Games

My wife says that many people in the church play religious "mind-games," trying to figure out why their faith or their prayers don't seem to be working. They want to find a reason why this person or that person is not healed, so they come up with excuses. "This person didn't have faith, or he must have some secret sin he won't confess." The games continue when the people in the church spend years casting out the same demon, claiming people are healed when they are still sick, or confessing a "healing" verse of Scripture repeatedly. In the end, all this fruitless speculation, and mental effort, heals no one, delivers no one, and makes no one whole. We may feel satisfied that we have explained why someone was not healed, but we have also made excuses for our failure to heal them. Perhaps you are lucky enough not to have encountered such strange and destructive religious thinking in your walk of faith, but many people I know are bound by such religious thinking.

Jesus rebuked his disciples when they tried to find a reason why a certain person was born blind. They asked, "Who sinned, this man or his parents, that he was born blind?" Jesus answered, "Neither, but it happened so that the glory of God could be revealed in him." [109] Jesus was really saying, "You are asking the wrong question! You shouldn't be asking 'Why this man is sick?' but 'How is God going to make him well?' You should be looking for

---

[109] John 9:2-3

solutions, not causes; for answers, not looking to place blame."

When Jesus healed, he healed the whole person. His primary concern was not why the person was sick, but seeing the person well. In dealing with the whole person, Jesus would deal with the causes. He would forgive sin, if sin were involved; cast out demons, if demons were the cause; and he would just heal them, if the sickness were without other cause. But, the Lord was not focusing his attention on what caused the disease; he was looking towards the cure in order to restore the health and well being of the person in need. It was compassion, which moved Jesus, not a desire to find a reason or to point the finger of blame. We shouldn't play mind-games either, or make excuses for ourselves. We ought to do the works that Jesus did, and heal them; or we should just keep our mouths shut.

Sanctify them in the truth: thy word is truth –John 17:17

So, what do you do if you don't have faith? It isn't a matter of getting more faith. It isn't a matter of quantity. It is a matter of truth. Jesus said, "You will know the truth and *the truth* will set you free."[110] It isn't faith alone that frees us, although we must know what and whom to believe; it is the truth which frees us. Believing the right things about God *will* set us free because it will sanctify us in the truth. We will be purified, cleansed, and made holy by the truth. What truth is it that sanctifies us? It is the truth of what God has done for us in Jesus Christ: he has already given us all the faith we will ever need.

Knowing Jesus, who is truth, will free us from error, darkness, sin and death. The truth is so powerful; it will free us from striving. We will cease struggling in our flesh to establish *our* faith, and we will allow God to establish *his* faith in us.

So, how does that apply to our fear that we do not have enough faith? The truth is: you already have enough faith. *All the faith you will ever need has already been given to you in Jesus Christ.* God

---

[110] John 8:32

has not left you lacking or needing anything. You do not need to grasp God's divine power and lay hold of it by your own strength or by the power of your mind. God has already given you what you need:

> *His divine power has given us everything we need for life and godliness through our knowledge of him who called us by his own glory and goodness. –2Peter 1:3, NIV*

Jesus, who lives in us, is God's faith at work in us. The problem is not that we don't have enough faith; the problem is: *we've been believing a lie.*

Chapter Nine

Escaping the Trap of Lies

To them God chose to make known how great among the Gentiles are the riches of the glory of this mystery, which is Christ in you, the hope of glory.   *–Colossians 1:27*

    The devil's strategy is to make you think you lack what is necessary for life and godliness. He wants to make you think you need something essential for your life, like faith, *which God has failed to provide.* It is the same lie the devil told to Adam and Eve in the Garden:

> Now the serpent was more subtle than any beast of the field which the LORD God had made. And he said unto the woman, "Yea, hath God said, Ye shall not eat of every tree of the garden?" And the woman said unto the serpent, "We may eat of the fruit of the trees of the garden: But of the fruit of the tree which is in the midst of the garden, God hath said, Ye shall not eat of it, neither shall ye touch it, lest ye die." And the serpent said unto the woman, "Ye shall not surely die: For God doth know that in the day ye eat thereof, then your eyes shall be opened, and ye shall be as gods, knowing good and evil." *–Genesis 3:1-5, KJV*

    Satan's tactic, in the beginning, was to make the people believe God was withholding something from them. He told them that eating the fruit would make them like gods. The truth was, Adam and Eve were already like God because they had been made in his "image and likeness!" The devil succeeded in making them believe a lie. The lie made them think God was depriving them of something good and necessary to life. The truth was: God had already given them everything they needed! He had already given them His likeness. By deceiving Adam and Eve, the devil caused them to believe a lie and so to fall.

Today, by making us believe we lack faith and that God has failed to give us the faith necessary for life and health, Satan has repeated his tactics of the Garden. He's lying again. Satan has made God seem distant and uncaring. God seems unwilling or unable to help us. So, rather than turn to God with confidence, we turn away from him in unbelief – or, in no-faith. We believe God will not answer us because we lack faith; so, we are left to our own devices. Satan's strategy hasn't changed since the beginning. It is still very effective. He makes us believe we cannot rely on God; we must rely on ourselves.

As I quoted in the last chapter, Peter says that God has *already* given us everything that is necessary for life and godliness. Faith is part of a godly character, so how could God give us all things necessary for godliness but neglect to give us faith? If he has given us all that is necessary for godliness, then he must also have given us faith! We may not feel like we have faith, or have enough faith, but that does not matter. The *truth* is we have faith. We lack nothing. We only need to be sanctified in the truth of what has been given to us in Jesus Christ. We need to stop being deceived by the devil and stop being tricked into believing his lies. And Satan's chief lie is this: Christ is not enough – you need something more than Jesus, and you must find it on your own.

Do you see how subtly the devil turns us from trust in God? It is not that we *cannot* trust God; it is that we are deceived into thinking that we cannot trust him. So, our faith is turned away from God towards another object. That object is a lie. We have all the faith we need, but we have directed our faith towards a lie. Satan's strategy shouldn't surprise us. He lives in deception and uses deception to mislead us. We have faith, but through deception, it is misdirected. Jesus said that the devil operates by using lies to hide the truth. Satan does his work by causing us to believe the lies he tells.

> *You belong to your father, the devil, and you want to carry out your father's desire. He was a murderer from the beginning, not holding to the truth, for there is **no truth** in him. When he lies, he speaks his native language, for he is a liar and the father of lies.* —John 8:44, NIV

The lie isn't a positive thing, but the absence of something. The lie is the absence of truth, and so our faith is shipwrecked when we believe the lies the devil tells. We are believing, but we are believing in the *wrong* thing.

In Deuteronomy, the Lord says the children of Israel who lack faith are a generation that is deceived by perversity:

> *And He said: "I will hide My face from them, I will see what their end will be, For they are a perverse generation, Children in whom is no faith."* —Deuteronomy 32:20, NKJV

The Hebrew word for "faith" is *amen*. It is the same word we say at the end of our prayers or sing at the end of our songs. But, the Hebrew word *amen* literally means "truth." So, when the children of Israel were deceived, they lacked faith because they had *no truth*. A lie caused them to have *no faith*. God's view is that truth will sanctify us, and faith will be the result; but if we have no faith, it is because we are without truth. God's remedy, then, is to teach us the truth which leads to faith.

What is the Truth?

What is truth? The truth is not a thing. The truth is a person. Jesus is the *"way, the truth and the life,"* (John 14:6). He is our truth. To know him is to know *the* truth. Jesus, then, is also the source of our faith, because faith comes from truth. Our faith comes from him. We do not believe from our own strength. We do not create faith within us. Our faith and our truth come from Jesus who lives within us. We are established by the faith he gives us. It is *his* faith working through us. All the faith we will ever need is already present with us, because Jesus' faith is perfect. He already believes the Father completely. Since God is within us, by the Holy Spirit, all the faith we need is present already to us.

You see, we have made a mistake looking for faith in our natural abilities, in our wisdom, and in our knowledge. Faith is not a product of the soul (of the mind, the heart, or the will). Faith does not come to us or work in us by the power of reason or by knowing what God has said on the pages of a book.[111] Faith is the work of God's presence in us. His Spirit communicates to our spirit, and so we believe and have faith. That is why Jesus is called the "author and finisher of our faith."[112] Jesus is the source and the creator of faith. Faith isn't something we have separately from Jesus; our faith flows out from him. It is Jesus in us, who believes the Father perfectly, who is manifesting *his faith* in us and through us. Because he is perfect in faith, we have all the faith we will ever need. Of course, we will grow in maturity. As we grow in the knowledge of the truth, our trust in him is perfected, and the truth will set us free.

Faith is a Gift of Communion

It has often been said that our fellowship with God is like respiration. We breathe in and out the Holy Spirit in a type of living communion with God. It isn't the body's natural breathing. We are talking about something spiritual – a relationship between ourselves and God. Just as breathing requires a constant flow, so our fellowship with God is a living thing. Faith is part of that spiritual respiration. It comes to us through communion with him. It isn't something we have on our own.

Faith also is a gift to us because it is part of the divine nature. God has faith; it is part of his being. It is part of who he is. The only way we can partake of it is if we receive it from God; for we could never create what is divine through our natural abilities! Faith cannot come to us by the power of the soul or by power of

---

[111] You search the scriptures, because you think that in them you have eternal life; and it is they that bear witness to me; yet you refuse to come to me that you may have life. (John 5: 39,40, RSV)
[112] Hebrews 12:2

human reason. Faith is part of the uncreated nature of God, and it is his gift to us:

> For by grace you have been saved through faith, and that not from yourselves; it is the gift of God. −Ephesians 2:8

When God gives us of himself, he gives us his faith.

Summary

To escape the snare of the enemy, we need to walk in the revelation of what God has *already* done for us. We don't need more faith; we need to be instructed in the truth of our faith, which is already complete in Christ. God has already given us everything that pertains to life and godliness. He has given us everything we need. Truth will break the yoke of deception, so that our faith will come to rest in God. ❦

Chapter Ten

Faith Comes by Healing!

May the God of peace himself sanctify you wholly; and may your spirit and soul and body be kept sound and blameless at the coming of our Lord Jesus Christ.
-1 Thessalonians 5:22,23, RSV

But God, who is rich in mercy, out of the great love with which he loved us, even when we were dead through our trespasses, made us alive together with Christ (by grace you have been saved), and raised us up with him, and made us sit with him in the heavenly places in Christ Jesus, that in the coming ages he might show the immeasurable riches of his grace in kindness toward us in Christ Jesus. For by grace you have been saved through faith; and this is not your own doing, it is the gift of God– not because of works, lest any man should boast. For we are his workmanship, created in Christ Jesus for good works, which God prepared beforehand, that we should walk in them. *-Ephesians 2:4-10, RSV*

The seed is sown; the ground prepared; but the growth comes from Almighty God ...

I wish I could give you a formula for established faith, but I cannot. I can only tell you a little of my journey towards wholeness. I write to you not as one who has arrived, but as a fellow traveler, still on the way.

One thing I know: it is not my faith that heals me or makes me whole. Not by *my* might or by *my* power, but by God's Spirit, is my faith perfected in the Father above. I am thankful that my healing depends upon God, who is my healer, rather than upon me. As the Scriptures say above, God is working in me to sanctify me and make me whole. I am his work; I am not my own creation.

It seems to me that God has allowed me to make many mistakes on my journey to find him. I have held onto the promise and the hope of knowing his perfected love through many years of being a Christian. While there have been many peaks and many valleys, it has taken almost 30 years to find the level plain, where my foot will not slip. I think God allows these struggles for a purpose. In the book of Judges, it says that God left enemies in the Promised Land to teach succeeding generations how to make war.[113] It was not good to let the generations grow fat and lazy. Conflict produces something within us. By causing us to seek God and call out to him, obstacles in our path draw us closer to him. I am told that if you help a chick break out of its shell, that baby chicken will weaken and die. Something in the struggle to break free from its eggshell causes it to become strong enough to weather the storms of life. It should be enough for us to know that God has ordained our struggles to perfect our faith and trust in him. However, being only human, we may often feel we have been abandoned to the winds of chaos by a God who is not in control of our destiny. Such thoughts remove our comfort and raise fears in our mind, which create a devil's playground within us. Nevertheless, we have a word from the Lord that God has allowed the conflict to teach us to war in the Spirit, so that we might grow strong in him and find victory through him. God – Father, Son, and Holy Spirit – is working to perfect us in the image and likeness of Jesus, that we might resemble him in every way.

I often look at Abraham and consider what he went through to become the father of faith. He heard from God that God would give him lands and children, but it was more than 30 years before the promise of the true son was fulfilled. During that time, Abraham struggled with doubt and unbelief, cowardice and counterfeits. Abraham tried to fulfill God's promise by natural human abilities. He had a son by a slave and named him Ishmael. He struggled to know God's promise fulfilled in his life; but only after he came to the end of himself did God step in with a supernatural blessing and fulfillment. Only after his own body was "as good as dead" and Sarah, his wife, had gone through menopause, did God step onto

---

[113] Judges 3:1-2

the scene. Abraham's faith was perfected in God when he had no other alternative and had given up all earthly hopes for his desire being fulfilled. The struggle God allowed, and which Abraham endured, brought Abraham to the place where he had no other alternative but to trust completely in God's word.[114]

Paul also talks of a season in his life where the times were so bad he despaired of life itself. Paul said it was for this purpose: "to make us rely not upon ourselves, but upon God who raised the dead ..."[115] God was perfecting Paul's trust in the extreme troubles he faced.

If God is the Craftsman and Workman who is making us into his likeness, then God's sovereign hand is at work perfecting us. God is above the struggles, using the conflicts to teach us to be victorious. While the conflicts may surround us, the battle is for our mind, heart, and soul. The circumstances we face may cause us to "despair of life itself," as did Paul, but the purpose is inward: to perfect our trust, so that we might rely fully upon God. Paul says, in fact, that the battle is not with this world's earthly powers, but with "mental reasonings and barriers of pride which resist the knowledge of God." In this conflict, his objective is to "take every thought captive so that it might obey Christ."[116] The harassments we endure may be external, but the victory is internal, as we come to the obedience of faith through the knowledge of God. Our thoughts will be held captive by Jesus Christ and be made to obey and believe him and his truth.

Healing by Faith

When you realize that Jesus has given you himself in the Holy Spirit, and because he is in you, you now have faith, it will soon dawn on you that you already have enough faith to be healed. Jesus is your healer, and he has the power at work within you to make you whole. You have the faith to be healed. As you realize you need nothing more from God to be made whole, it will change your prayers and your expectations. Paul desires us to know what it is that God has done for us. He understands that it is not a matter

---

[114] Genesis, Chaps. 11 - 22
[115] 2 Corinthians 1: 8-9
[116] 2 Corinthians 10:5-6

of more power, but of greater revelation:

> *I do not cease to give thanks for you, remembering you in my prayers, that the God of our Lord Jesus Christ, the Father of glory, may give you a spirit of wisdom and of revelation in the knowledge of him, having the eyes of your hearts enlightened, that you may know what is the hope to which he has called you, what are the riches of his glorious inheritance in the saints, and what is the immeasurable greatness of his power in us who believe, according to the working of his great might ... –Ephesians 1:16-19, RSV*

Why did Paul think it was important for us to have revelation? He knew that if we really understood the incredible power of God already available to us, it would change our lives. We would no longer see ourselves as beggars begging crumbs of bread and mercy; we would see ourselves as agents of the King of Kings, who are already "seated" on the throne with Christ in heavenly places, "far above all rule and authority and power and dominion" of this earth.[117] We are to look down on the problems of this earth as those who rule and reign with Christ, not as cripples under the dominion of the powers of this age. When we see our position in Christ, we will have faith, and rather than beg God for healing, we will command the devil to leave us alone. A ruler doesn't beg subjects to do his bidding; he commands them to do his will or else suffer the consequences. Jesus spoke to the demons; they obeyed immediately. If we are seated in heavenly places with Christ, then how are we to respond to the demons which are already "under" Jesus' feet and ours?

There is a reason our thoughts must be taken captive by Christ. If we do not see ourselves as ruling and reigning over spiritual principalities and powers, we cannot very well command them with faith. If we are believing the lie that we are still under the power of the elemental spirits of this world, we will act like we are powerless. Our thoughts must be taken captive by the knowledge of God to be able to know the truth and to act upon it.

---

[117] Ephesians 1:21 & 2:6.

Damaged Hearts, Broken Minds

The Spirit of the Lord GOD is upon me, because the LORD has anointed me to bring good tidings to the afflicted; he has sent me to bind up the brokenhearted, to proclaim liberty to the captives, and the opening of the prison to those who are bound; to proclaim the year of the Lord's favor, and the day of vengeance of our God; to comfort all who mourn ...
– Isaiah 61:1,2, RSV

There are many impediments to faith within us. Often, the way we have been raised or the wounds we have received have distorted our picture of God. People who have suffered physical or sexual abuse often feel that God has abandoned them. They may have developed a picture of a distant God who does not care about them. Such a picture of God is the result of a real experience in the world. The experience was true – it really happened – but the picture of God that resulted is not. It has become a stronghold in the mind; a little area where Satan has set up a fort of lies to twist the mind into a distorted view of God.

Sometimes, in order for us to be able to believe God, we need to be healed. Our picture of God needs to be recreated, and the wounds that caused our pain need to be bound up by Christ. We need to be set free from our captivity by the love of Jesus. If the wound is deep, it might not heal itself. It might require the hand of the Shepherd, a vial of oil, and some thread to stitch the wound. Deep wounds require so great a love that the love of redemption becomes more real to us than the pain of our affliction. God's love can wipe away the memory and the sorrow of any injustice and reverse the curses of our existence. Sometimes, a deep work is required to heal us, so that we may believe.

I have spoken earlier of the need to forgive. Forgiveness is a powerful tool, which can release great changes in our life. Forgiving others is a first step on the road to our own healing. There really is no limit to the effects of forgiveness, and it is necessary to forgive those who, in times present or past, have caused us harm. However, the process of healing is so individual and complex, that each of you must come to know God for yourself in your situation. You have to break out of your own eggshell. The revelation of his might and power must become real *to you*. It is part of the mystery of God that he expresses his great love for you and reaches you where you are.

While forgiveness is a major part of the healing process, sometimes people are so hurt and damaged they do not know what is wrong with them. They may need counseling or help from a pastor or friend to get perspective on their situation. They may need help uncovering the roots of their discomfort in order to be freed from their distress. If you need such counsel, do not be ashamed, but seek it out from reputable ministries, which are committed to Christ and to the Scriptures. This kind of counsel and help is beyond the scope of this book, but when your heart and mind are restored and healed, believing God becomes natural to you. It isn't something you have to force; it is something that becomes second nature. Faith indeed comes by being healed; for when you are healed, you know how much God loves you, and because you know his love, it is easy to believe good things about God.

Since you are unique in God's site, I won't pretend I have a prescription to bring healing to your mind and heart. I will tell you a little of my journey, so that you may see how pulling down strongholds of the mind leads to faith.

My father and I love each other very much, but we are very different people. I am more like my mother in interests and values than my father. My father is an orthopedic surgeon who did well in science. My mother is an artist. I have a flair for art and creative activities. I have always been interested in philosophy and theories. When I was growing up, I really wasn't interested in making money, because I really did not want many things. As I grew up, my father became concerned that I was becoming impractical in my outlook towards life and money, and perhaps he feared I'd grow up without ambition and not be responsible to look after myself. Somewhere in my teen years, he said to me, "Don't ever ask me for money." I don't think that thought ever crossed my mind, but when he said that, it impacted me in a way beyond anything he ever intended.

I later became a Christian in my college years, and although I read the Scriptures where Jesus tells us to "ask and you shall receive," I had an inner block to these words. Even though the Scriptures tell us to ask God for things and believe we will receive them, inwardly and unconsciously I projected my father's words upon God. Subconsciously, my inner mind told me that I was not allowed to ask God for anything. To ask God in prayer for any help was a sign of failure. "Don't ever ask me for money," became translated in my inner mind, "Don't ever ask me (God, your heavenly Father), for help. If you do, you are a failure."

Psychologists tell us that, as children, our earthly role models often shape our image of God. Even if we know better from reading the Scriptures, our unconscious mind plays tricks on us. We hold a deep, inner thought that is contrary to what God says in his Word, and it is impossible for us to believe God fully. Although we want to believe, there is thought, a stronghold of the mind, which resists the knowledge of God. Such thoughts as these need to be taken captive to release us into a life of unhindered faith.

I went to talk to a pastoral counselor who helped me see how I had unconsciously projected my encounter with my father onto my image of God. I could not help but be double-minded in my prayers, because deep within myself, I was negating every prayer I made. By asking God for help, I was proving my lack of worth and proving myself a failure. Such a perverted way of looking at things may seem strange to you, but that is a perfect example of how Satan uses deceptions to create strongholds of the mind which rob us of our intimacy with God. We need to be healed of these misconceptions and these lies, so that we come to the place where we may believe God and treat our prayers to God with the confidence they have been heard.

May you also find the healing of heart and mind that I am finding on my walk towards Jesus Christ. May your faith be perfected as mine is being made complete.

Chapter Eleven

The Goal of the Christian Life

And Enoch lived sixty and five years, and begat Methuselah: And Enoch walked with God after he begat Methuselah three hundred years, and begat sons and daughters: And all the days of Enoch were three hundred sixty and five years: And Enoch walked with God: and he was not; for God took him.
–Genesis 5:21-24, KJV

It says in Proverbs, "without a vision, the people perish," (29: 18). People without direction are subject to all sorts of destructive winds because they do not know the will of God for their lives. If sickness or disease comes, rather than pray in faith for healing, they may endure the ravages of cancer without prayer, thinking God sent it to teach them or punish them. They interpret the attack of Satan as God's will, and so, they submit to the devil when they should resist him.

Jesus never gave anybody cancer, sickness, or disease, but he healed everyone who came to him.[118] Jesus was the perfect revelation of God's will. He was the perfect will of God for creation. He is so much like the Father in every respect – in will, desire, and purpose – that he said, "He who has seen me, has seen the Father."[119] Jesus considered sickness and disease part of Satan's kingdom, a kingdom he came to destroy.[120] When Jesus touched the sick they were delivered into wholeness, and he said: "If I drive out demons by the Spirit of God, then the kingdom of God has come upon you," (Matt. 12:28). According to Jesus, *the sign* of the kingdom of God *is* healing and deliverance. Sickness is a sign of the devil's rule. Religious traditions teach that God gives us diseases to teach us something, but Jesus never gave anyone a disease. He never said, "Here, I'm making you sick to teach you something. I won't tell you what it is, but it will help you grow." Jesus didn't

---

[118] Matthew 4:24; 12:15
[119] John 14:9
[120] Matthew 12: 22–29, Acts 10:38

do that. He healed the sick and made them whole. The example of Jesus is the perfect revelation of God's will for us, and we can pray accordingly.

Can you see how our faith would be inoperative if we did not know that God wanted us well? We would pray in uncertainty and double-mindedness, not sure what God would do. But Jesus said if we "believe and do not doubt" in our heart, then we will receive the object of our prayer.[121] For this reason, we should not let a lack of vision prevent us from entering the Promised Land of God's rest.

So then, what is the goal of life in Christ while here on the earth? What is God trying to do in us, through us, and for us? We are to be conformed to the image of Jesus, but that is too general a description to give us much direction for our lives. *The goal of our life in Christ Jesus is to walk in such intimacy and unbroken fellowship with God that, like Enoch, we walk in heaven while still on the earth. So close are we to be to God that even the barrier of distinction between heaven and earth becomes indistinct to us. We become so wrapped up in the presence of Jesus that we cross back and forth between these two realms in the Spirit.* The elders of Israel had a foretaste of this when they ate with God the Father in the heavenlies.[122] They ate with God at the heavenly table, and the pavement stones were like sapphires beneath their feet. God desires this heavenly fellowship with his Church.

A lot of religious people tend to look at the saints of God in the New and Old Testaments and say to themselves "I could never be like so and so because I'm so unworthy," or something like that. But listen to this: Enoch was a man who didn't even have the Holy Spirit dwelling on the inside of him, yet he grew so close to God in fellowship that he did not suffer death. Instead, he was translated right into heaven. If Enoch had that type of relationship with God, could we have it too?

Jesus said, "I tell you the truth: Among those born of women there has not risen anyone greater than John the Baptist; yet

---

[121] Mark 11:23

[122] Moses and Aaron, Nadab and Abihu, and the seventy elders of Israel went up and saw the God of Israel. Under his feet was something like a pavement made of sapphire, clear as the sky itself. But God did not raise his hand against these leaders of the Israelites; they saw God, and they ate and drank. (Exodus 24:9–11, NIV)

he who is least in the kingdom of heaven is greater than he," (Matt. 11: 11). Jesus said that of all the Old Testament saints, the measliest, weakest person who is born of the Spirit of God is greater than them all! You – if you have the Spirit of God in you – are greater than all those who went before. More can be done in you and through you than any of those who lived before the Holy Spirit was given, because the Spirit of the Living God now dwells within you. God himself is in your flesh! Therefore, if it was possible for Enoch, that great old saint, to walk in unbroken fellowship, it is also possible for you. Not only is it possible, but God desires it for you. And God is able to bring it to pass in your life, and he will, if you allow him. Faith is necessary to this walk; for God will ask you to trust him as he purifies you in the truth of what he has done for you in Jesus Christ.

Whether we perceive it or not, the unbroken fellowship we have in Christ Jesus is already spiritual truth. The blood of Jesus has purchased for us that relationship. God continually makes us sinless through the blood of Christ. Yet, we still need to come into the awareness of that truth and make it a reality by faith. Though the Promised Land had been given to the children of Israel, they did not have the faith to walk into the land and take possession of it. God gave it to them, but they did not believe. It may sound too good to be true to you also. Perhaps you have a hard time believing that God wants you to walk with him in heavenly places like Enoch. It should fill your heart with hope and joy that such a thing might be possible. However, you could turn your back on such a great and precious promise, just as the Israelites did when they came to the borders of the Promised Land. Then God waited for the next generation to go in and take possession of the promise. Our faith is part of the maturity God requires of us, and by it, he holds us accountable. He has shown us by the example of Enoch that the promised land of intimacy and rest awaits us.

There is a reason for the testing and trying of our faith. God wants to perfect our faith in him and to mature us in our expectation so that as we walk towards him, we have the confidence of a great inheritance available to us in this life. However, it is important to know that this intimacy with God is not contingent upon our being perfect. It is not necessary for us to be without sin in our natural selves. Enoch sinned. What God provided in the sacrifice of Jesus was the end of sin's power to divide us from the presence of God. Our sins, no matter how many, are washed away. When we sin, now by the blood of the Lamb, we do not have to fear God as Adam did. Rather, we can come to God without fear, knowing that he has already forgiven us. Sin's power to divide us from God is broken. Each time we sin, we can run to God and not away from him. Therefore, we can enter that intimate communion with God, as Enoch did, without needing to be, nor pretending to be, perfect. In spite of our sin, we can walk in that unbroken fellowship through Jesus. Hallelujah!

Chapter Twelve

The Goal of Sanctification

May God himself, the God of peace, sanctify you through and through. May your whole spirit, soul and body be kept blameless at the coming of our Lord Jesus Christ.
—1 Thessalonians 5:23, NIV

The goal of sanctification is not sinlessness but relationship. If sinlessness comes, if that is even possible in this life for us, it is a byproduct of our intimacy with Jesus. The idea of perfection as some ideal state of being does not make sense in Hebraic thinking. The idea of a static perfection comes from a Greek philosophical background. Perfection in the Christian sense is one of relationship: unbroken fellowship with God. If you walk with God, then you are perfected in love for God and for others.[123] The attempt to reach some sinless state of static perfection is really just sin disguised. It is the flesh trying once again to be so good and holy that it has no need to be dependent upon God for righteousness. Our perfection, if you want to call it that, is Christ. Our real perfection is a walk of intimacy that is so deep that our love for God and love for others becomes our reason for being. Perfection in love is possible according to John, but perfect love is a living, breathing relationship with God who is perfect love.[124] It is not something we have separate from him residing in us. It is not some kind of ethical perfection, where we never think wrong thoughts, have wrong desires, or lose our temper. God puts his perfect love in us and casts out our fear of judgment and our fear of sin. He, by his love, removes our fear of facing him and confessing our transgressions.

One of the problems with the idea of Christian perfection, aside from our philosophical heritage, is the fact that the word *perfection*

---

[123] 1 John 1:6; 3: 14 & 15; 4: 16–21
[124] 1 John 4: 17–18

in Greek does not mean what it does in English. Perfection in Greek is the word *telos*, which means "the purpose" or "the completion." It might be better translated as "maturity." When love is perfected in us, it is not that we never sin; it means that love is made complete or completely mature in us. It has fulfilled its purpose in our lives. We have fulfilled the purpose of our creation. So, in love, we do not become perfectly sinless; what happens is that we have learned to walk in love towards others even when they treat us poorly. Even when persecuted, we do not hate them in return, but we have learned not to respond in kind. Perfected love responds to persecution with more love. That kind of "perfection" is not only possible, but also God's desire for us in Creation. His purpose is that we become like Jesus, and how better do we resemble him than if we walk in love?

> But I say unto you, Love your enemies, bless them that curse you, do good to them that hate you, and pray for them which despitefully use you, and persecute you; That ye may be the children of your Father which is in heaven: for he maketh his sun to rise on the evil and on the good, and sendeth rain on the just and on the unjust. For if ye love them which love you, what reward have ye? do not even the publicans the same? And if ye salute your brethren only, what do ye more than others? do not even the publicans so? Be ye therefore perfect, even as your Father which is in heaven is perfect.
> – Matthew 5: 44-48, KJV

If you want to be perfect, don't seek it outside of Christ. Don't seek it outside of intimacy with Jesus. The closer you grow to Jesus, the less you will care about finding any righteousness in yourself at all. His righteousness is enough. You will find all your concern is with his love for you, and the issue of perfection will become a light concern. When you look to yourself, you will quickly abandon that attention and look back to Jesus because he has all the righteousness you will ever need. He is so worthy. He is so good. Why trouble yourself with your imperfection before his holiness? Your sin is forgiven and washed away by the blood of his sacrifice.

If you seek anything, seek to grow into the awareness and likeness of his love, that you may be consumed with the joy of his presence. Let love be your aim, and by faith, believe that God has this for you. He has sanctified you for himself. He requires nothing of you except that you believe in him and in the One whom he has sent. He paid the price for your sin and he purchased your sanctification, so that in his eyes you might be holy and blameless – without spot, wrinkle, or blemish. He washed you in the blood of his Son, that you might be seen as if you have never sinned. Amen!

Chapter Thirteen

God My Sanctifier

Grain must be ground to make bread; so one does not go on threshing it for ever. Though he drives the wheels of his threshing-cart over it, his horses do not grind it. All this also comes from the LORD Almighty, wonderful in counsel and magnificent in wisdom.
–Isaiah 28:28-29, NIV

I want to make sure that I do not leave you with the naive impression that because of your faith, you will never suffer. As I said, we are called to endure persecution for Christ's sake. As a matter of fact, the Scriptures guarantee we **will** suffer persecution if we are faithful to Jesus.[125] Faith brings the persecution of this world, because the world hates God and resists Jesus who is in us. God does not will that people hate us; his desire is that they receive Jesus and be saved, but he also knows people's hearts. He knows that some will not receive the Word of Life. But because he loves the sinner and because he his faithful to himself, he will not leave the people without a witness to his own nature and compassion. Our Father is even willing to let us be sacrificed for the sake of the lost, so great is his compassion towards them. For he knows that even their hatred and resistance can at times be overcome by the demonstration of his divine patience and love in and through us.

And he has committed to us the message of reconciliation. We are therefore Christ's ambassadors, as though God were making his appeal through us. We implore you on Christ's behalf: Be reconciled to God. –2 Corinthians 5:19-20, NIV

In spite of humanity's resistance to God, he still sends us as living epistles to a fallen and hostile world. It is as if God is crying out to them through us, "Stop fighting Me and fear no more; be

---

[125] In fact, everyone who wants to live a godly life in Christ Jesus will be persecuted, (2 Timothy 3:12, NIV). Remember the words I spoke to you: `No servant is greater than his master.' If they persecuted me, they will persecute you also ... (John 15:20, NIV).

reconciled to Me and find peace and forgiveness through My Son." He does this knowing, even then, some will persist in their rejection of his love.

God gives freedom to the creatures of his image, and when they use that freedom to hate and persecute, it looks like God is out of control of his creation. To the degree that he allows us to choose evil and to do evil, he has in a sense relinquished some control over us. But he has never yielded his sovereignty. Things happen that he permits, but which he does not desire. There is a limit, however, to what he will permit to happen on the earth. He sets a limit to our rebellion and our ability to do damage to one another. Yet, he is willing to endure far more rebellion from his creation than most of us would, because his love is greater and his hope is more profound than ours. He knows that many who appear to be lost forever will indeed repent and turn to him.

It does not take much knowledge of history to see the depths of depravity to which the human race descends from time to time. The Holocaust, Stalin, Pol Pot's purges of millions, the slaughter of millions of unborn children, rape, and violence in our streets, all testify to the terrible consequence of misspent human freedom. It speaks of the terrible price the creation pays for our rebellious freedom and willful rejection of God. Yet, God has permitted things he does not desire. And he permits great evil for the sake of his love for fallen humanity.

What then of us who believe? Like being thrown to pack of raging wolves, are we at the mercy of the chaos of God's creation? No, not at all – although it may appear that way to us from time to time. No, God's sovereign hand of protection is upon us as well, and he will not let us suffer beyond what he has determined, and only that which serves his purpose.[126] Remember that God's purpose may be twofold: one, he loves the people who have set themselves against us, and he hopes to reach them through us;

---

[126] No temptation has seized you except what is common to man. And God is faithful; he will not let you be tempted beyond what you can bear. But when you are tempted, he will also provide a way out so that you can stand up under it. (1 Corinthians 10:13, NIV)

and two, he also has a plan for our lives, and he can work, even in the evil that others do, to bring some good in our lives.[127] I know what I am saying may be hard to accept and seem contrary to what I have shared before, but notice I am not implying that sickness and disease are part of God's plan, but I am saying that he may call us to endure human rejection and resistance from time to time as *part of his plan!* God can use persecution as his means of birthing in us character and maturity, which resemble the perfect character of his dear son Jesus.

God is not stupid. Even though we are sanctified by faith and remade in the image of God by the indwelling Holy Spirit, our growth into the maturity of faith, our sanctification if you will, is not an intellectual process. God has a hand on our character, and like a master sculptor, he is chipping away at those defects of personality, which are marks of our immaturity and unbelief. We are fallen creatures, whose personalities have been affected by sin, selfishness, and unbelief. That fact creates a real need within us for renewal of the soul. The effect of unbelief is sin. Impatience, greed, anger, jealousy, and all other marks of the flesh, reveal the areas of our personality which need to be healed. God is not fooled by our good theology. In spite of our understanding, there exist within us defects of character, which do not reflect the divine and perfect nature of his son Jesus. God is able to use the circumstances of evil in this world as his chisel to strike away at our indifference, our insensitivity, our lack of love, our impatience, and our unbelief.

Can you really love your enemies? If you are put in a situation of persecution, can you love them like Christ does? Jesus told us that in order to be perfect, like our Father in Heaven, we must also love our enemies and pray for those who persecute us.[128] How great is your love? Can you love those who abuse and use you? Can you forgive them? The Scripture says that by enduring persecution, we can become more like God.[129] Paul said that suffering persecution

---

[127] And we know that in all things God works for the good of those who love him, who have been called according to his purpose. (Romans 8:28, NIV)

[128] Matthew 5: 43–48

brought him closer to Jesus:

> *What is more, I consider everything a loss compared to the surpassing greatness of knowing Christ Jesus my Lord, for whose sake I have lost all things. I consider them rubbish, that I may gain Christ and be found in him, not having a righteousness of my own that comes from the law, but that which is through faith in Christ-the righteousness that comes from God and is by faith.* **I want to know Christ and the power of his resurrection and the fellowship of sharing in his sufferings, becoming like him in his death,** *and so, somehow, to attain to the resurrection from the dead.*
> –Philippians 3:8-11, NIV

Paul says he will become like Christ *by sharing in the persecution that Jesus suffers.* He will come to know Jesus better by experiencing the rejection Jesus suffered, and he will know better the love Jesus had for lost humanity by enduring the same rejection Christ endured. Paul implies that intimacy with God comes by partaking of the same afflictions which Jesus suffered on behalf of creation. What higher a calling is there then than sharing in our Lord's passion and compassion for humanity? In what other way could our love grow more if not by sharing Jesus' sorrow, as he endures hurt and rejection through us?

You might ask, "How then are we going to know when it is God's will for us to suffer the effects of persecution and when it is his will for us to escape them?" That is a good question, and I am afraid I don't have an answer for this one. It will depend upon your intimacy with the Father and upon knowing his will for you in a specific situation. It will also depend upon your maturity and your previous suffering. I know early in my life I had a persecution complex, believing I was supposed to suffer all the time. That attitude was not from Christ; it was a little masochistic. Even in service to God, suffering will be balanced with joy. I suppose if your suffering causes you an increase in bitterness, then perhaps it is not all inspired by God; or at least your response to suffering is

---

[129] James 1: 2–4

not inspired by God. Jesus endured people's hatred, but he always had the confidence that his Father loved him. The persecution he endured never was able to shake his confidence in the Father, except perhaps when he was enduring the cross itself and was abandoned by the Father to death.

Jesus was hated, but he knew his Father loved him. He could discern between the rejection of men and the purposes of God. He did not submit to every rejection as the Father's will for his life. When people wanted to throw him over a cliff, he walked through their midst unscathed. Although they wanted to kill him, they could not touch him.[130] He knew when and where he was to suffer, and he did not receive harm until that time.[131] If we look at Paul, he remarks how often he was beaten and how much he endured for Christ's sake,[132] yet Jesus told him in advance his sufferings were part of God's plan for his life:

> *But the Lord said to Ananias, "Go! This man is my chosen instrument to carry my name before the Gentiles and their kings and before the people of Israel. I will show him how much he must suffer for my name." –Acts 9:15-16, NIV*

Paul had some idea of what he was called to endure as part of his obedience to Christ. Yet, he also escaped many times in his ministry, being warned by disciples and friends of attempts on his life.[133] Jesus also told Peter how he would end his life. Peter was to be crucified just like his master.[134] Yet, Peter twice escaped from prison by a miracle when Satan wanted to destroy Peter's life before the Lord's time.[135]

If we are sensitive to the Spirit's leading, we also may know when suffering has been appointed to us and when it is just an attack of the devil to be resisted by faith and prayer. We do not always have the luxury of knowing such things in advance. Sometimes the storms of life are incomprehensible to us as we are going through them, and only later, as the dark clouds and raging winds give way to sunlit calm, do we understand the hand of the Lord was

---

[130] Luke 4: 28–30
[131] Luke 13: 31–33
[132] 2 Cor. 11: 24–28
[133] Acts 9: 25; Acts 14:20
[134] John 21: 18–19
[135] Acts 5 & 12

in the midst of our circumstance. Sometimes, we must hang onto the knowledge that our Father loves us and is in control of our circumstances, especially when our faith does not seem up to the task of our deliverance.

Sometimes also, God allows us to go through these rough seas because he wants us to grow up and respond in faith, rebuke the winds, and fight the good fight of faith. For it says, "Submit yourselves, then, to God. Resist the devil, and he will flee from you," (James 4:7, NIV). Peter also says the same thing:

> *Be self-controlled and alert. Your enemy the devil prowls around like a roaring lion looking for someone to devour. Resist him, standing firm in the faith, because you know that your brothers throughout the world are undergoing the same kind of sufferings. And the God of all grace, who called you to his eternal glory in Christ, after you have suffered a little while, will himself restore you and make you strong, firm and steadfast. –1 Peter 5:8-10, NIV*

There are times, it seems, when God requires of us a faith for battle and for war; when our obedience should issue forth in resistance to the devil and his physical and emotional attempts at torment. Faith for deliverance is required in these circumstances. I also believe that there are situations and circumstances that the Lord will not deliver us from until we have responded to God in faith:

> *In this you greatly rejoice, though now for a little while you may have had to suffer grief in all kinds of trials. These have come so that your faith-of greater worth than gold, which perishes even though refined by fire-may be proved genuine and may result in praise, glory and honor when Jesus Christ is revealed. –1 Peter 1:6-7, NIV*

It seems that our Father will use trials to cause our faith to come to maturity. Even persecution may be used to bring our faith to adulthood. It takes discernment to know how to respond to these various circumstances. On some occasion, God may ask us to give our lives away in faith, trusting God with eternity and an unseen future life. Or, if we are beaten for our love of Christ, perhaps our faith is to be shown in our confidence that God will heal us and deliver us from the physical consequences of that abuse. On other occasions, God may give us the grace to escape the persecution. In Revelation, God told the church in Philadelphia that he would spare them from the hour of trial that was coming on the face of the whole earth because of their faithful endurance of past suffering.[136]

I am sorry that I don't have a pat and easy answer to such a difficult question. I wish there was one. But I believe this is an area where there are no formulas. This knowledge is dependent upon your wisdom and maturity in the Lord. I would also recommend that you get the counsel of believing friends and your pastor if the situations that you face seem impenetrable to you. By prayer and faith, let them help you discern the will of God for your life in these circumstances. Even if your faith seems to be failing, as mine has many times when trying to fight off sickness or disease, remember that there "is no longer any condemnation for those who are in Christ Jesus."[137] So, even if your faith is weak, there is no reason to fall under condemnation because of it. Don't let your failures, if indeed they are your failures, divide you from the love of God in Christ Jesus. Don't let the devil make an accusation about your sin and then use your failure as a wedge to divide you from the Father who has forgiven you.

Persecution and Joseph

Most of the persecution we endure today in the United States is not physical affliction but emotional persecution. Some of us lose employment, but few of us are beaten or murdered because of our faith in Jesus Christ. Even when Jesus walked through the midst of the angry mob in Nazareth, he escaped the consequence of the people's anger, but he did not escape the fact that he was hated. Neither will we. So as faithful servants of Christ Jesus, we can, at the very least, expect to be misunderstood, mocked, ridiculed, and persecuted socially for our faith and confession of Jesus Christ as Lord. Therefore, be prepared and be willing to endure these things

---

[136] Rev. 3: 7–10
[137] Romans 8:1

for Christ's sake.

Even in the midst of the suffering we endure at the hands of others, who, in the heat of anger, press for our destruction, recognize that God still has a hand over and above our circumstances. He desires not only the maturity of our faith, but also the perfection of our character. He uses even the evil that men may do to us for our own good. I can think of no better example of this pattern of God's master plan for our maturity than Joseph. Joseph, as a young boy, was given a dream by God. In that dream, God revealed Joseph would rule over his brothers and even over his mother and father.[138] Joseph received the word of God to him in faith and with faith. He believed the word. However, Joseph was not wise or mature. He should have kept these matters to himself. Instead, he bragged about his dream to his brothers, who were already jealous of him because of their father, who favored Joseph. To boast in front of his brothers was not a smart thing to do! Bragging is not a sign of a love, but of immaturity. The problem wasn't Joseph's faith; it was his character. God still loved him. The promises and dreams were still true, but God had a lot of work to do with Joseph before those good plans could be fulfilled.

The same is true for you and me. There are areas of our character which do not reflect Christ. We are often blind to our own imperfections, but our Lord clearly sees our need. He arranges circumstances and situations to expose and confront our imperfection, that through the trials we might be conformed to the image of Jesus. God is sovereignly at work, orchestrating the circumstances of our lives to test the Word at work in us and to prove our character. He has a plan for us just as he did for Joseph.

After Joseph had this dream and bragged about it, his brothers conspired against him, threw him into a pit, and sold him into slavery. For about 13 years, Joseph was in and out of prison, suffered unjust persecution, and was tried and tested in the furnace of affliction. In all that time, God was working on the man and preparing him for a position of authority and power. After 13 years,

---

[138] See Genesis 37–47

Joseph's dream finally started to come true. He was exalted to be the governor of all Egypt, second in command only to Pharaoh. In that time of affliction, Joseph had gained the humility of heart, the patience, and the wisdom to execute authority without it going to his head. He was no longer prideful by the time that God was done with him. And when his brothers, father, and stepmothers finally did come down to Egypt to escape a famine, they did bow down to Joseph as to a governing king, as the dream foretold. However, Joseph did not boast; instead, he cried tears of joy to see his family again! God had a plan for Joseph and part of that plan was years of suffering. Part of the plan was the delay and temporary denial of the promises of God. Joseph was 17 when he received the promise, but he was 37 when the dream finally was fulfilled. In between, Joseph spent years in suffering and persecution. These years were also part of God's plan for Joseph's life. The promise was not denied; it was not delayed. God timed the fulfillment to Joseph's maturity. He would not fulfill it before Joseph had been prepared to receive it.

This time of testing, to which we are all subjected, tells us that God is more interested in our maturity and character than he is in fulfilling all our material needs, wants, and desires. He is willing to delay the fulfillment of prosperity in order to prepare our hearts to worship him first and above all.[139] Our material needs are temporal, but our character is eternal. God is big enough that he can delay even the promises he has given until such a time as we are ready to receive them. He has a much larger plan for our lives than satisfying all our immediate desires.

To understand God's purpose will give us a sustaining vision. If we don't have a picture of God's sovereignty in all these trials; if we don't realize that these trials have a purpose and are not a mistake; if we don't see that God is bigger than our circumstances, we will be too easily discouraged. Our vision of God will not be big enough to cope with the difficulties we go through as part of the process of preparation for victory.

Joseph's testimony was this: "You intended to harm me, but God

---

[139] He humbled you, causing you to hunger and then feeding you with manna, which neither you nor your fathers had known, to teach you that man does not live on bread alone but on every word that comes from the mouth of the LORD. (Deuteronomy 8:3, NIV)

intended it for good ..." (Genesis 50:20, NIV). Yes, God had a plan. He also has a plan for us. Even in the face of evil and resistance, we are not the victims of our circumstances. Even in the face of the apparent success of evil schemes, God has a plan, and that plan is for our good! No schemes of the devil can prosper over the plan of God – if we are walking in obedience before God. If we are seeking the will of the Lord, even the obstacles we face are part of the plan of God for our maturity and our victory. The persecutions and imprisonments are part of God's charter of victory for us. How we respond to the testing will often determine the length of the trial. If we respond by grumbling rather than believing God's ultimate purpose and good for us, then we may spend longer in the test that God would normally require. Yet, even then, if we repent, God may send forth our deliverance speedily.

Character Before Promotion

So, not only does God have a plan for perfecting our faith, he also has a plan for perfecting our character. He desires that we not only walk in the likeness of his faith, but also that we walk in the likeness of his love:

> *Beloved, since God loved us so much, we also ought to love one another ... There is no fear in love, but perfect love casts out fear; for fear has to do with punishment, and whoever fears has not reached perfection in love. We love because he first loved us. Those who say, "I love God," and hate their brothers or sisters, are liars; for those who do not love a brother or sister whom they have seen, cannot love God whom they have not seen. The commandment we have from him is this: those who love God must love their brothers and sisters also. –1 John 4:11, 18-21, NRSV*

Without God's divine love conforming our character to his, then all the faith in the world is of no advantage to us. That faith would be prideful and vain. It would have power but no intimacy with God. Jesus warned against those who have faith but no relationship with him:

On that day many will say to me, 'Lord, Lord, did we not prophesy in your name, and cast out demons in your name, and do many deeds of power in your name?' Then I will declare to them, 'I never knew you; go away from me, you evildoers.' –Matthew 7:22-23, NRSV

God does not want us to walk in power without also walking in the character of Christ. He wants us to be a living expression of his son Jesus, both in deed and in attitude, and he will not rest until that character is fully formed in us.

God has a plan for our lives! Can you trust him to work his work in your life? Can you trust him when you are going through struggles and conflicts that you cannot understand? He is concerned with the sanctification of your character. That is why he is called "The Lord my Sanctifier," because he sees our needs and our weaknesses better than we do ourselves. He knows just what we need to become more like him. He is the master craftsman working in the midst of our circumstances to sanctify us and make us more like himself.[140] He is our sanctifier. He is the one who makes us holy. He is the one who brings us to maturity. We do not sanctify ourselves. He has his hand on our lives, and he has our lives in his hand.

You are God's Poetry

The good news is that God is not creating a piece of machinery; he is creating a work of art. The Scripture says, "we are his workmanship, created in Christ Jesus unto good works, which God hath before ordained that we should walk in them," (Ephesians 2:10, KJV). The word "workmanship" in Greek is *poiema,* from which we get our English word "poetry." We are God's poetry. We are works of beauty which he is creating for his glory and pleasure, and he will not allow us to be less than he has desired. Like the master potter, he is using the circumstances of our lives – our loves and friendships, our pastors and teachers, our schools and churches, our jobs and recreation, even our hardships and trials – as his

---

[140] Keep my statutes, and observe them; I am the LORD; I sanctify you. (Leviticus 20:8, NRSV). You yourself are to speak to the Israelites: "You shall keep my sabbaths, for this is a sign between me and you throughout your generations, given in order that you may know that I, the LORD, sanctify you. (Exodus 31:13, NRSV)

means of removing the mars from our character and of shaping our souls into the likeness of Jesus.

But know this: the suffering is not intended to go on forever. After the cross comes the resurrection, and after patient endurance comes fulfillment. God's ultimate plan is for the fulfillment of the dreams and visions he has planted in our hearts.[141] He doesn't crush our personality forever, but after he has kneaded us, he bakes us into a loaf of his fulfilled purpose.[142] Joseph's imprisonment was only for a season, then the ultimate plan of God was fulfilled in his life; he was exalted to be Governor of Egypt. So also, the stress and testing we endure to perfect our faith and our character are only meant to last for a season. God has a plan for fulfillment, and if we will walk in obedience before him and not grumble or lose heart, then we will see the purposes of God revealed in our lives. So we should have this confidence towards him and not fear God's plan: "For surely I know the plans I have for you, says the LORD, plans for your welfare and not for harm, to give you a future with hope," (Jeremiah 29:11, NRSV). Just as the Scripture says, "many are the afflictions of the righteous, but the Lord, he delivers him from them all," [143] so we should also have confidence that God's plan is for our victory, not for our defeat and destruction.

As you walk in him and become like him, expect also his deliverance. Do not take obstacles and difficulties as God's judgment of you, but as opportunities he has provided for your growth in the likeness of him:

> *...therefore my brothers and sisters, consider it a joyful thing when you encounter various trials; knowing this, that the testing of your faith works to make you persistent. And let persistence work its full effect in you, that you may be perfect and completely mature, lacking absolutely nothing.*
> *–James 1:2-4.*

So rejoice in all things, for if you do this, you will have passed the test.

Finally, as you walk towards this goal of maturity in Christ

---

[141] Psalm 37
[142] Isaiah 28: 28–29
[143] Psalm 34:19

Jesus, you can expect intimacy with him even now. You do not need to wait until you are perfected to dwell in his presence. The storms of life will draw you into his presence. You may have love and fellowship with him right now, even while your character is being perfected under God's mighty hand. It is this intimacy with Jesus, which allows his perfect love to become a part of us. Our nearness to him allows his love to flow out in response to the difficult circumstances we face. The presence of Jesus is the means of our perfection and the method of our healing. We are sanctified by him!

Being near to him, we learn to respond like him in love. By abiding in his presence, faith will overcome doubt, love will overcome fear, victory will replace defeat, and patience will have its perfect work in us. God will, through trials and tests, perfect us in his love as we draw near to him. Through faith and patience, we will overcome the obstacles of life. We may even receive the fulfillment of the dreams and desires he has planted in our heart. Though we are not perfect in ourselves, we have fellowship with the God of the Universe, and as we enter his presence, his presence will sanctify us!

Amen ~ Truth!

Appendix

A Summary Doctrine of Sanctification

1) God Alone is Righteous and God alone is Good:

Only in the LORD, it shall be said of me, are righteousness and strength; to him shall come and be ashamed, all who were incensed against him, (Isaiah 45:24, RSV).

And Jesus said to him, "Why do you call me good? No one is good but God alone," (Luke 18:19, RSV).

2) We are not to look to ourselves for any good or righteousness, for none exists in us:

For I know that nothing good dwells within me, that is, in my flesh, (Romans 7:18, RSV).

For, being ignorant of the righteousness that comes from God, and seeking to establish their own, they did not submit to God's righteousness, (Romans 10:3, RSV).

Indeed I count everything as loss because of the surpassing worth of knowing Christ Jesus my Lord. For his sake I have suffered the loss of all things, and count them as refuse, in order that I may gain Christ and be found in him, not having a righteousness of my own, based on law, but that which is through faith in Christ, the righteousness from God that depends on faith; (Philippians 3:8-9, RSV).

3) The only righteousness we have is Jesus Christ in us:

He is the source of your life in Christ Jesus, whom God made our wisdom, our righteousness and sanctification and redemption; therefore, as it is written, "Let him who boasts, boast of the Lord," (1 Corinthians 1:30-31, RSV).

4) We are saved, not because of any good deeds on our part, but through faith:

For by grace you have been saved through faith; and this is not your own doing, it is the gift of God-not because of works, lest any man should boast, (Ephesians 2:8-9,

RSV).

So do not be ashamed to testify about our Lord, or ashamed of me his prisoner. But join with me in suffering for the gospel, by the power of God, who has saved us and called us to a holy life-not because of anything we have done but because of his own purpose and grace. This grace was given us in Christ Jesus before the beginning of time, (2 Timothy 1:8-9, NIV).

Now we know that whatever the law says, it says to those who are under the law, so that every mouth may be silenced and the whole world held accountable to God. Therefore no-one will be declared righteous in his sight by observing the law; rather, through the law we become conscious of sin, (Romans 3:19-20, NIV).

For we hold that a man is justified by faith apart from works of law, (Romans 3:28, RSV).

5) **We are sanctified, made holy, not by good works, but also by that same faith, for Christ is not only God's righteousness in us-he is also the One who is perfect in us:**

" ...delivering you (Paul) from the people and from the Gentiles-to whom I send you to open their eyes, that they may turn from darkness to light and from the power of Satan to God, that they may receive forgiveness of sins and a place among those who are sanctified by faith in me," (Acts 26:17-18, RSV).

O foolish Galatians! Who has bewitched you, before whose eyes Jesus Christ was publicly portrayed as crucified? Let me ask you only this: Did you receive the Spirit by works of the law, or by hearing with faith? Are you so foolish? Having begun with the Spirit, are you now ending with the flesh? Did you experience so many things in vain? – if it really is in vain. Does he who supplies the Spirit to you and works miracles among you do so by works of the law, or by hearing with faith? (Galatians 3:1-5, RSV)

...Christ Jesus, whom God made our ...sanctification, (1 Corinthians 1:30-31, RSV).

...in order that the just requirement of the law might be fulfilled in us, who walk not according to the flesh but according to the Spirit, (Romans 8:4, RSV).

But you are not in the flesh, you are in the Spirit, if in fact the Spirit of God dwells in you. Any one who does not have the Spirit of Christ does not belong to him, (Romans 8:9, RSV).

6) **Sanctification then is not something we achieve, it is something that we receive. Sanctification is God's work, for he is the One who makes us Holy:**

Do not profane my holy name. I must be acknowledged as holy by the Israelites. I am the LORD, who makes you holy, (Leviticus 22:32, NIV).

You shall not profane my holy name, that I may be sanctified among the people of Israel: I am the LORD; I sanctify you, (Leviticus 22:32, NRSV).

7) **We grow in Christ's likeness, not through good works, but through growing in our trust in Jesus and his all sufficient work for us. As we trust his work for us more completely and trust him in all things, we rest in him. As we rest in him by faith, he pours his nature into us:**

Thou dost keep him in perfect peace, whose mind is stayed on thee, because he trusts in thee, (Isaiah 26:3, RSV).

So then, there remains a sabbath rest for the people of God; for whoever enters God's rest also ceases from his labors as God did from his. Let us therefore strive to enter that rest, that no one fall by the same sort of disobedience, (Hebrews 4:9-11, RSV).

And we all, with unveiled face, beholding the glory of the Lord, are being changed into his likeness from one degree of glory to another; for this comes from the Lord who is the Spirit, (2 Corinthians 3:18, RSV).

8) **As we grow in trust in him, our character becomes more like his, and good works are produced naturally, as an expression of our relationship to him. They are the**

byproduct of relationship, not the cause of it nor the means to gain relationship:

> Abide in me, and I in you. As the branch cannot bear fruit by itself, unless it abides in the vine, neither can you, unless you abide in me. I am the vine, you are the branches. He who abides in me, and I in him, he it is that bears much fruit, for apart from me you can do nothing, (John 15:4-5, RSV).

> I am speaking in human terms, because of your natural limitations. For just as you once yielded your members to impurity and to greater and greater iniquity, so now yield your members to righteousness for sanctification, (Romans 6:19, RSV).

9) As we walk in the knowledge of our own transgression and of our lack of worthiness based upon our good deeds, we will know that we have been saved only by God's goodness, His mercy, and His Grace. Because of that knowledge of our unworthiness, we will be much less likely to judge others and much more likely to extend mercy, grace, and compassion, and in so doing, we will begin to express more completely the character of Christ and so become more like Jesus:

> But love your enemies, and do good, and lend, expecting nothing in return; and your reward will be great, and you will be sons of the Most High; for he is kind to the ungrateful and the selfish. Be merciful, even as your Father is merciful. Judge not, and you will not be judged; condemn not, and you will not be condemned; forgive, and you will be forgiven ... (Luke 6:35-37, RSV).

> Above all hold unfailing your love for one another, since love covers a multitude of sins, (1 Peter 4:8, RSV).

> For judgment is without mercy to one who has shown no mercy; yet mercy triumphs over judgment, (James 2:13, RSV).

> Blessed are the merciful, for they shall obtain mercy, (Matthew 5:7, RSV).

10) **Righteousness and sanctification come through relationship to the Father; not through our efforts. We are established in relationship by faith and trust in Jesus' finished work on the Cross.**

Therefore, since we have been justified through faith, we have peace with God through our Lord Jesus Christ, through whom we have gained access by faith into this grace in which we now stand. And we rejoice in the hope of the glory of God, (Romans 5:1-2, NIV).

However, to the man who does not work but trusts God who justifies the wicked, his faith is credited as righteousness, (Romans 4:5, NIV).

11) **Therefore, we can continually confess and face our actual sin, because we are free of the need to have any righteousness in ourselves.**

If we say we have no sin, we deceive ourselves, and the truth is not in us. If we confess our sins, he is faithful and just, and will forgive our sins and cleanse us from all unrighteousness. If we say we have not sinned, we make him a liar, and his word is not in us, (1 John 1:8-10, RSV).

Therefore confess your sins to one another, and pray for one another, that you may be healed. The prayer of a righteous man has great power in its effects, (James 5:16, RSV).

12) **Our righteousness is Christ and He alone. He is our Sanctification, our Sanctifier! He is the Holy One who lives inside us. It is He that is holy within us, not our flesh. Our righteousness is not something we have independently from God, as if it were our character. Our righteousness is the Holy God who lives within us by His Spirit.**

Do you not know that you are God's temple and that God's Spirit dwells in you? If any one destroys God's temple, God will destroy him. For God's temple is holy, and that temple you are, (1 Corinthians 3:16-17, RSV).

Do you not know that your body is a temple of the Holy

Spirit within you, which you have from God? You are not your own; you were bought with a price. So glorify God in your body, (1 Corinthians 6:19-20, RSV).

Follow the pattern of the sound words which you have heard from me, in the faith and love which are in Christ Jesus; guard the truth that has been entrusted to you by the Holy Spirit who dwells within us, (2 Timothy 1:13-14, RSV).

Only in the LORD, it shall be said of me, are righteousness and strength; to him shall come and be ashamed, all who were incensed against him, (Isaiah 45:24, RSV).

For I know that nothing good dwells within me, that is, in my flesh, (Romans 7:18, RSV).

For, being ignorant of the righteousness that comes from God, and seeking to establish their own, they did not submit to God's righteousness, (Romans 10:3, RSV).

Indeed I count everything as loss because of the surpassing worth of knowing Christ Jesus my Lord. For his sake I have suffered the loss of all things, and count them as refuse, in order that I may gain Christ and be found in him, not having a righteousness of my own, based on law, but that which is through faith in Christ, the righteousness from God that depends on faith; (Philippians 3:8-9, RSV).

About the Author

Jefferis Kent Peterson has been a pastor since 1984, graduating from Wesley Theological Seminary in Wash. D.C. with a Master of Divinity. He served in the Presbyterian Church (USA) until 1990. He left there join a non-denominational fellowship and eventually became vice-president of the network called Antioch International Ministries. For several years, he served on the board of a local crisis pregnancy center, and, from 1995-1999, he and his wife, Leigh, worked in am outreach ministry in Slippery Rock, PA.

Jeff is also a businessman. In addition to working in sales and marketing since 1990, he is a pioneer on the Web, creating one of the first Christian courses for the Internet and publishing an online magazine in 1994.

Jeff launched his own web design studio in 1998 (www.PetersonSales.net). When not writing, he is engaged full time in graphic design and internet animation. He now resides in Western Pennsylvania with Leigh, who is a school teacher.

For speaking or ministry engagements, please contact:
Isaiah House Publishers
PO Box 56
Erie, PA 16512-0056
(814) 452-1152
or email to: Jefferis@ScholarsCorner.com

Also Available from
Isaiah House Publishing

Victory in the Battle
by
John Kowalczyk

Video Tapes
Manuals & Cassettes
&
Other Ministry Resources
from

Isaiah House Publishing
http://www.is61.com
PO Box 56
Erie, PA, 16512-0056

(814) 452-1152

More about:

Victory in the Battle

by John Kowalczyk

Why do so many Christians live defeated lives? When the Bible promises them healing and deliverance, why are Christians some of the most oppressed, diseased, and dysfunctional people on earth? Where is the God of healing and wholeness who will give them a new life in Christ - a life which will make them want to witness and tell others about the good things God has done for them?

This book is about the Key to Victory. The Key to Victory is hearing God's voice in the midst of your battles. If you hear His voice in your struggle, you will find victory every time.

ISBN: #0-9718079-1-4

Isaiah House Publishing
http://www.is61.com
PO Box 56
Erie, PA, 16512-0056
(814) 452-1152

for
Theological Debate & Cultural Critiques - visit:

The Scholar's Corner

Viewing Contemporary Culture Through the Eyes of Christ. Comparing Popular Culture, Christian Perspectives, and a Biblical Worldview. Providing a Critique of Pop culture, analyzing secular trends, the media, and Western Worldviews.

join
The RoundTable
an online discussion group
sponsored by

The Scholar's Corner
http://www.ScholarsCorner.com
at
www.ScholarsCorner.com/welcome/contact.htm

look for future releases by

Jefferis Kent Peterson:

*The Fallacy of the Mustard Seed:
an Examination of the Misconceptions about
Faith*

*You Are a Holy of Holies –
Why You Are Priest of the Most High God*

*Shepherd and the Sheep:
Perspectives from Pulpit & Pew*

*Faith or Fatalism:
Examining the Difference between
Providence & a Divine Whim*

SUGGESTED READING LIST:

On the dynamic relationship between law and grace in a life of holiness:

Paul and the Law: A Contextual Approach – by Frank Thielman, InterVarsity Press, 1994.

The Faith of Jesus Christ : The Narrative Substructure of Galatians 3:1-4:11 (The Biblical Resource Series) – by Richard B. Hays, Luke Timothy Johnson, Eerdmans Publishing Co., 2001.

On contemporary culture:

All God's Children and Blue Suede Shoes: Christians & Popular Culture - by Kenneth A. Myers, Turning Point Christian Worldview, 1989.

The Scandal of the Evangelical Mind - by Mark Noll, Eerdmans Publishing Co., 1994.

On New Testament government:

Wisdom Hunter – by Randall Arthur, Multnomah Publishers, 1999, (A novel with a great example of a healthy church).

I Will Build My Church – by A. John Carr, Charis Publications, Dundee, Scotland, 1992.

PARDONED OR PAROLED?

Notes

PARDONED OR PAROLED?

Notes